Author's National Edition

THE WRITINGS OF
MARK TWAIN
Volume III

This is the authorized
Uniform Edition of all
my books.

Mark Twain

SUNRISE AT MOUNT RIGA

A TRAMP ABROAD

BY
MARK TWAIN
(SAMUEL L. CLEMENS)

IN TWO VOLUMES
VOL. I

ILLUSTRATED

HARPER & BROTHERS PUBLISHERS
NEW YORK AND LONDON

CONTENTS

A TRAMP ABROAD

A TRAMP ABROAD

CHAPTER I

ONE day it occurred to me that it had been many years since the world had been afforded the spectacle of a man adventurous enough to undertake a journey through Europe on foot. After much thought, I decided that I was a person fitted to furnish to mankind this spectacle. So I determined to do it. This was in March, 1878.

I looked about me for the right sort of person to accompany me in the capacity of agent, and finally hired a Mr. Harris for this service.

It was also my purpose to study art while in Europe. Mr. Harris was in sympathy with me in this. He was as much of an enthusiast in art as I was, and not less anxious to learn to paint. I desired to learn the German language; so did Harris.

Toward the middle of April we sailed in the *Holsatia*, Captain Brandt, and had a very pleasant trip, indeed.

After a brief rest at Hamburg, we made preparations for a long pedestrian trip southward in the soft spring weather, but at the last moment we changed

MARK TWAIN

the program, for private reasons, and took the express-train.

We made a short halt at Frankfort-on-the-Main, and found it an interesting city. I would have liked to visit the birthplace of Gutenberg, but it could not be done, as no memorandum of the site of the house has been kept. So we spent an hour in the Goethe mansion instead. The city permits this house to belong to private parties, instead of gracing and dignifying herself with the honor of possessing and protecting it.

Frankfort is one of the sixteen cities which have the distinction of being the place where the following incident occurred. Charlemagne, while chasing the Saxons (as *he* said), or being chased by them (as *they* said), arrived at the bank of the river at dawn, in a fog. The enemy were either before him or behind him; but in any case he wanted to get across, very badly. He would have given anything for a guide, but none was to be had. Presently he saw a deer, followed by her young, approach the water. He watched her, judging that she would seek a ford, and he was right. She waded over, and the army followed. So a great Frankish victory or defeat was gained or avoided; and in order to commemorate the episode, Charlemagne commanded a city to be built there, which he named Frankfort—the ford of the Franks. None of the other cities where this event happened were named from it. This is good evidence that Frankfort was the first place it occurred at.

Frankfort has another distinction—it is the birthplace of the German alphabet; or at least of the German word for alphabet—*Buchstaben*. They say that the first movable types were made on birch sticks—*Buchstabe*—hence the name.

I was taught a lesson in political economy in Frankfort. I had brought from home a box containing a thousand very cheap cigars. By way of experiment, I stepped into a little shop in a queer old back street, took four gaily decorated boxes of wax matches and three cigars, and laid down a silver piece worth 48 cents. The man gave me 43 cents change.

In Frankfort everybody wears clean clothes, and I think we noticed that this strange thing was the case in Hamburg, too, and in the villages along the road. Even in the narrowest and poorest and most ancient quarters of Frankfort neat and clean clothes were the rule. The little children of both sexes were nearly always nice enough to take into a body's lap. And as for the uniforms of the soldiers, they were newness and brightness carried to perfection. One could never detect a smirch or a grain of dust upon them. The street-car conductors and drivers wore pretty uniforms which seemed to be just out of the bandbox, and their manners were as fine as their clothes.

In one of the shops I had the luck to stumble upon a book which has charmed me nearly to death. It is entitled *The Legends of the Rhine from Basle to Rotterdam*, by F. J. Kiefer; translated by L. W. Garnham, B.A.

All tourists *mention* the Rhine legends—in that sort of way which quietly pretends that the mentioner has been familiar with them all his life, and that the reader cannot possibly be ignorant of them—but no tourist ever *tells* them. So this little book fed me in a very hungry place; and I, in my turn, intend to feed my reader, with one or two little lunches from the same larder. I shall not mar Garnham's translation by meddling with its English; for the most toothsome thing about it is its quaint fashion of building English sentences on the German plan—and punctuating them according to no plan at all.

In the chapter devoted to "Legends of Frankfort," I find the following:

"THE KNAVE OF BERGEN

"In Frankfort at the Romer was a great mask-ball, at the coronation festival, and in the illuminated saloon, the clanging music invited to dance, and splendidly appeared the rich toilets and charms of the ladies, and the festively costumed Princes and Knights. All seemed pleasure, joy, and roguish gaiety, only one of the numerous guests had a gloomy exterior; but exactly the black armor in which he walked about excited general attention, and his tall figure, as well as the noble propriety of his movements, attracted especially the regards of the ladies. Who the Knight was? Nobody could guess, for his Vizier was well closed, and nothing made him recognizable. Proud and yet modest he advanced to the Empress; bowed on one knee before her seat, and begged for the favor of a waltz with the Queen of the festival. And she allowed his request. With light and graceful steps he danced through the long saloon, with the sovereign who thought never to have found a more dexterous and excellent dancer. But also by the grace of his manner, and fine conversation he knew to win the Queen, and she graciously accorded him a second dance for which he begged, a third, and a fourth, as well as others were not refused him. How all regarded the happy dancer, how many envied him the high favor; how increased curiosity, who the masked knight could be.

"Also the Emperor became more and more excited with curiosity, and with great suspense one awaited the hour, when according to mask-law, each masked guest must make himself known. This moment came, but although all others had unmasked; the secret knight still refused to allow his features to be seen, till at last the Queen driven by curiosity, and vexed at the obstinate refusal; commanded him to open his Vizier. He opened it, and none of the high ladies and knights knew him. But from the crowded spectators, 2 officials advanced, who recognized the black dancer, and horror and terror spread in the saloon, as they said who the supposed knight was. It was the executioner of Bergen. But glowing with rage, the King commanded to seize the criminal and lead him to death, who had ventured to dance, with the queen; so disgraced the Empress, and insulted the crown. The culpable threw himself at the feet of the Emperor, and said—

"'Indeed I have heavily sinned against all noble guests assembled here, but most heavily against you my sovereign and my queen. The Queen is insulted by my haughtiness equal to treason, but no punishment even blood, will not be able to wash out the disgrace, which you have suffered by me. Therefore oh King! allow me to propose a remedy, to efface the shame, and to render it as if not done. Draw your sword and knight me, then I will throw down my gauntlet, to every one who dares to speak disrespectfully of my king.

_."The Emperor was surprised at this bold proposal, however it appeared the wisest to him; 'You are a knave he replied after a moment's consideration, however your advice is good, and displays prudence, as your offense shows adventurous courage. Well then, and gave him the knight-stroke, so I raise you to nobility, who begged for grace for your offense now kneels before me, rise as knight; knavish you have acted, and Knave of Bergen shall you be called henceforth, and gladly the Black knight rose; three cheers were given in honor of the Emperor, and loud cries of joy testified the approbation with which the Queen danced still once with the Knave of Bergen."

CHAPTER II

WE stopped at a hotel by the railway-station. Next morning, as we sat in my room waiting for breakfast to come up, we got a good deal interested in something which was going on over the way, in front of another hotel. First, the personage who is called the *portier* (who is not the *porter*, but is a sort of first-mate of a hotel)[1] appeared at the door in a spick-and-span new blue cloth uniform, decorated with shining brass buttons, and with bands of gold lace around his cap and wristbands; and he wore white gloves, too. He shed an official glance upon the situation, and then began to give orders. Two women - servants came out with pails and brooms and brushes, and gave the sidewalk a thorough scrubbing; meanwhile two others scrubbed the four marble steps which led up to the door; beyond these we could see some men-servants taking up the carpet of the grand staircase. This carpet was carried away and the last grain of dust beaten and banged and swept out of it; then brought back and put down again. The brass stair-rods received an exhaustive polishing and were returned to their places. Now a troop of servants brought pots and

[1] See Appendix A.

7

tubs of blooming plants and formed them into a
beautiful jungle about the door and the base of the
staircase. Other servants adorned all the balconies
of the various stories with flowers and banners;
others ascended to the roof and hoisted a great flag
on a staff there. Now came some more chamber-
maids and retouched the sidewalk, and afterward
wiped the marble steps with damp cloths and finished
by dusting them off with feather brushes. Now a
broad black carpet was brought out and laid down
the marble steps and out across the sidewalk to the
curbstone. The *portier* cast his eye along it, and
found it was not absolutely straight; he commanded
it to be straightened; the servants made the effort—
made several efforts, in fact—but the *portier* was
not satisfied. He finally had it taken up, and then
he put it down himself and got it right.

At this stage of the proceedings, a narrow bright
red carpet was unrolled and stretched from the top
of the marble steps to the curbstone, along the
center of the black carpet. This red path cost the
portier more trouble than even the black one had
done. But he patiently fixed and refixed it until it
was exactly right and lay precisely in the middle of
the black carpet. In New York these performances
would have gathered a mighty crowd of curious and
intensely interested spectators; but here it only
captured an audience of half a dozen little boys,
who stood in a row across the pavement, some with
their school-knapsacks on their backs and their
hands in their pockets, others with arms full of
bundles, and all absorbed in the show. Occasionally

one of them skipped irreverently over the carpet and took up a position on the other side. This always visibly annoyed the *portier*.

Now came a waiting interval. The landlord, in plain clothes, and bareheaded, placed himself on the bottom marble step, abreast the *portier*, who stood on the other end of the same steps; six or eight waiters, gloved, bareheaded, and wearing their whitest linen, their whitest cravats, and their finest swallow-tails, grouped themselves about these chiefs, but leaving the carpetway clear. Nobody moved or spoke any more but only waited.

In a short time the shrill piping of a coming train was heard, and immediately groups of people began to gather in the street. Two or three open carriages arrived, and deposited some maids of honor and some male officials at the hotel. Presently another open carriage brought the Grand Duke of Baden, a stately man in uniform, who wore the handsome brass-mounted, steel-spiked helmet of the army on his head. Last came the Empress of Germany and the Grand Duchess of Baden in a closed carriage; these passed through the low-bowing groups of servants and disappeared in the hotel, exhibiting to us only the backs of their heads, and then the show was over.

It appears to be as difficult to land a monarch as it is to launch a ship.

But as to Heidelberg. The weather was growing pretty warm,—very warm, in fact. So we left the valley and took quarters at the Schloss Hotel, on the hill, above the Castle.

Heidelberg lies at the mouth of a narrow gorge—a gorge the shape of a shepherd's crook; if one looks up it he perceives that it is about straight, for a mile and a half, then makes a sharp curve to the right and disappears. This gorge—along whose bottom pours the swift Neckar—is confined between (or cloven through) a couple of long, steep ridges, a thousand feet high and densely wooded clear to their summits, with the exception of one section which has been shaved and put under cultivation. These ridges are chopped off at the mouth of the gorge and form two bold and conspicuous headlands, with Heidelberg nestling between them; from their bases spreads away the vast dim expanse of the Rhine valley, and into this expanse the Neckar goes wandering in shining curves and is presently lost to view.

Now if one turns and looks up the gorge once more, he will see the Schloss Hotel on the right, perched on a precipice overlooking the Neckar—a precipice which is so sumptuously cushioned and draped with foliage that no glimpse of the rock appears. The building seems very airily situated. It has the appearance of being on a shelf half-way up the wooded mountainside; and as it is remote and isolated, and very white, it makes a strong mark against the lofty leafy rampart at its back.

This hotel had a feature which was a decided novelty, and one which might be adopted with advantage by any house which is perched in a commanding situation. This feature may be described as a series of glass-inclosed parlors *clinging to the outside of the house*, one against each and every bed-chamber and drawing-room. They are like long, narrow, high-ceiled bird-cages hung against the building. My room was a corner room, and had two of these things, a north one and a west one.

From the north cage one looks up the Neckar gorge; from the west one he looks down it. This last affords the most extensive view, and it is one of the loveliest that can be imagined, too. Out of a billowy upheaval of vivid green foliage, a rifle-shot removed, rises the huge ruin of Heidelberg Castle,[1] with empty window arches, ivy-mailed battlements, moldering towers—the Lear of inanimate nature—deserted, discrowned, beaten by the storms, but royal still, and beautiful. It is a fine sight to see the evening sunlight suddenly strike the leafy declivity at the Castle's base and dash up it and drench it as with a luminous spray, while the adjacent groves are in deep shadow.

Behind the Castle swells a great dome-shaped hill, forest-clad, and beyond that a nobler and loftier one. The Castle looks down upon the compact brown-roofed town; and from the town two pictur-esque old bridges span the river. Now the view broadens; through the gateway of the sentinel head-lands you gaze out over the wide Rhine plain, which stretches away, softly and richly tinted, grows gradually and dreamily indistinct, and finally melts imperceptibly into the remote horizon.

I have never enjoyed a view which had such a serene and satisfying charm about it as this one gives.

[1] See Appendix B.

The first night we were there, we went to bed and to sleep early; but I awoke at the end of two or three hours, and lay a comfortable while listening to the soothing patter of the rain against the balcony windows. I took it to be rain, but it turned out to be only the murmur of the restless Neckar, tumbling over her dikes and dams far below, in the gorge. I got up and went into the west balcony and saw a wonderful sight. Away down on the level, under the black mass of the Castle, the town lay, stretched along the river, its intricate cobweb of streets jeweled with twinkling lights; there were rows of lights on the bridges; these flung lances of light upon the water, in the black shadows of the arches; and away at the extremity of all this fairy spectacle blinked and glowed a massed multitude of gas-jets which seemed to cover acres of ground; it was as if all the diamonds in the world had been spread out there. I did not know before, that a half-mile of sextuple railway-tracks could be made such an adornment.

One thinks Heidelberg by day—with its surroundings—is the last possibility of the beautiful: but when he sees Heidelberg by night, a fallen Milky Way, with that glittering railway constellation pinned to the border, he requires time to consider upon the verdict.

One never tires of poking about in the dense woods that clothe all these lofty Neckar hills to their tops. The great deeps of a boundless forest have a beguiling and impressive charm in any country; but German legends and fairy tales have given these an added charm. They have peopled all that region with gnomes, and dwarfs, and all sorts of mysterious and uncanny creatures. At the time I am writing of, I had been reading so much of this literature that sometimes I was not sure but I was beginning to believe in the gnomes and fairies as realities.

One afternoon I got lost in the woods about a mile from the hotel, and presently fell into a train of dreamy thought about animals which talk, and kobolds, and enchanted folk, and the rest of the pleasant legendary stuff; and so, by stimulating my fancy, I finally got to imagining I glimpsed small flitting shapes here and there down the columned aisles of the forest. It was a place which was peculiarly meet for the occasion. It was a pine wood, with so thick and soft a carpet of brown needles that one's footfall made no more sound than if he were treading on wool; the tree-trunks were as round and straight and smooth as pillars, and stood close together; they were bare of branches to a point about twenty-five feet above-ground, and from there upward so thick with boughs that not a ray of sunlight could pierce through. The world was bright with sunshine outside, but a deep and mellow twilight reigned in there, and also a silence so profound that I seemed to hear my own breathings.

When I had stood ten minutes, thinking and imagining, and getting my spirit in tune with the place, and in the right mood to enjoy the supernatural, a raven suddenly uttered a horse croak over my head. It made me start; and then I was angry because I started. I looked up, and the creature was sitting on a limb right over me, looking down at me. I felt something of the same sense of humiliation and injury which one feels when he finds that a human stranger has been clandestinely inspecting him in his privacy and mentally commenting upon him. I eyed the raven, and the raven eyed me. Nothing was said during some seconds. Then the bird stepped a little way along his limb to get a better point of observation, lifted his wings, stuck his head far down below his shoulders toward me, and croaked again—a croak with a distinctly insulting expression about it. If he had spoken in English he could not have said any more plainly than he did say in raven, "Well, what do *you* want here?" I felt as foolish as if I had been caught in some mean act by a responsible being, and reproved for it. However, I made no reply; I would not bandy words with a raven. The adversary waited a while, with his shoulders still lifted, his head thrust down between them, and his keen bright eye fixed on me; then he threw out two or three more insults, which I could not understand, further than that I knew a portion of them consisted of language not used in church.

I still made no reply. Now the adversary raised his head and called. There was an answering croak from a little distance in the wood—evidently a croak of inquiry. The adversary explained with enthusiasm, and the other raven dropped everything and came. The two sat side by side on the limb and discussed me as freely and offensively as two great naturalists might discuss a new kind of bug

The thing became more and more embarrassing. They called in another friend. This was too much. I saw that they had the advantage of me, and so I concluded to get out of the scrape by walking out of it. They enjoyed my defeat as much as any low white people could have done. They craned their necks and laughed at me (for a raven *can* laugh, just like a man), they squalled insulting remarks after me as long as they could see me. They were nothing but ravens—I knew that—what they thought about me could be a matter of no consequence—and yet when even a raven shouts after you, "What a hat!" "Oh, pull down your vest!" and that sort of thing, it hurts you and humiliates you, and there is no getting around it with fine reasoning and pretty arguments.

Animals talk to each other, of course. There can be no question about that; but I suppose there are very few people who can understand them. I never knew but one man who could. I knew he could, however, because he told me so himself. He was a middle-aged, simple-hearted miner who had lived in a lonely corner of California, among the woods and mountains, a good many years, and had studied the ways of his only neighbors, the beasts and the birds, until he believed he could accurately translate any remark which they made. This was Jim Baker. According to Jim Baker, some animals have only a limited education, and use only very simple words, and scarcely ever a comparison or a flowery figure; whereas, certain other animals have a large vocabulary, a fine command of language and a ready and

fluent delivery; consequently these latter talk a
great deal; they like it; they are conscious of their
talent, and they enjoy "showing off." Baker said,
that after long and careful observation, he had come
to the conclusion that the bluejays were the best
talkers he had found among birds and beasts. Said
he:

"There's more *to* a bluejay than any other creature. He has got more moods, and more different
kinds of feelings than other creatures; and, mind
you, whatever a bluejay feels, he can put into language. And no mere commonplace language, either,
but rattling, out-and-out book-talk—and bristling
with metaphor, too—just bristling! And as for
command of language—why *you* never see a bluejay
get stuck for a word. No man ever did. They
just boil out of him! And another thing: I've
noticed a good deal, and there's no bird, or cow,
or anything that uses as good grammar as a bluejay.
You may say a cat uses good grammar. Well,
a cat does—but you let a cat get excited once;
you let a cat get to pulling fur with another cat
on a shed, nights, and you'll hear grammar that
will give you the lockjaw. Ignorant people think
it's the *noise* which fighting cats make that is so
aggravating, but it ain't so; it's the sickening grammar they use. Now I've never heard a jay use bad
grammar but very seldom; and when they do, they
are as ashamed as a human; they shut right down
and leave.

"You may call a jay a bird. Well, so he is, in a
measure—because he's got feathers on him, and

don't belong to no church, perhaps; but otherwise
he is just as much a human as you be. And I'll
tell you for why. A jay's gifts, and instincts, and
feelings, and interests, cover the whole ground. A
jay hasn't got any more principle than a Congress-
man. A jay will lie, a jay will steal, a jay will
deceive, a jay will betray; and four times out of
five, a jay will go back on his solemnest promise.
The sacredness of an obligation is a thing which you
can't cram into no bluejay's head. Now, on top
of all this, there's another thing; a jay can out-
swear any gentleman in the mines. You think a cat
can swear. Well, a cat can; but you give a bluejay a subject that calls for his reserve-powers, and
where is your cat? Don't talk to *me*—I know too
much about this thing. And there's yet another
thing; in the one little particular of scolding—just
good, clean, out-and-out scolding—a bluejay can lay
over anything, human or divine. Yes, sir, a jay
is everything that a man is. A jay can cry, a jay
can laugh, a jay can feel shame, a jay can reason
and plan and discuss, a jay likes gossip and scandal,
a jay has got a sense of humor, a jay knows when
he is an ass just as well as you do—maybe better.
If a jay ain't human, he better take in his sign,
that's all. Now I'm going to tell you a perfectly
true fact about some bluejays."

CHAPTER III

" WHEN I first begun to understand jay language correctly, there was a little incident
happened here. Seven years ago, the last man in
this region but me moved away. There stands his
house—been empty ever since; a log house, with
a plank roof—just one big room, and no more; no
ceiling—nothing between the rafters and the floor.
Well, one Sunday morning I was sitting out here in
front of my cabin, with my cat, taking the sun, and
looking at the blue hills, and listening to the leaves
rustling so lonely in the trees, and thinking of the
home away yonder in the states, that I hadn't heard
from in thirteen years, when a bluejay lit on that
house, with an acorn in his mouth, and says,
'Hello, I reckon I've struck something.' When he
spoke, the acorn dropped out of his mouth and
rolled down the roof, of course, but he didn't care;
his mind was all on the thing he had struck. It
was a knot-hole in the roof. He cocked his head to
one side, shut one eye and put the other one to the
hole, like a possum looking down a jug; then he
glanced up with his bright eyes, gave a wink or two
with his wings — which signifies gratification, you
understand—and says, 'It looks like a hole, it's lo-

18

cated like a hole—blamed if I don't believe it *is* a hole!'

"Then he cocked his head down and took another look; he glances up perfectly joyful, this time; winks his wings and his tail both, and says, 'Oh, no, this ain't no fat thing, I reckon! If I ain't in luck!—why it's a perfectly elegant hole!' So he flew down and got that acorn, and fetched it up and dropped it in, and was just tilting his head back, with the heavenliest smile on his face, when all of a sudden he was paralyzed into a listening attitude and that smile faded gradually out of his countenance like breath off'n a razor, and the queerest look of surprise took its place. Then he says, 'Why, I didn't hear it fall!' He cocked his eye at the hole again, and took a long look; raised up and shook his head; stepped around to the other side of the hole and took another look from that side; shook his head again. He studied a while, then he just went into the *de*tails—walked round and round the hole and spied into it from every point of the compass. No use. Now he took a thinking attitude on the comb of the roof and scratched the back of his head with his right foot a minute, and finally says, 'Well, it's too many for *me*, that's certain; must be a mighty long hole; however, I ain't got no time to fool around here, I got to 'tend to business; I reckon it's all right—chance it, anyway.'

"So he flew off and fetched another acorn and dropped it in, and tried to flirt his eye to the hole quick enough to see what become of it, but he was too late. He held his eye there as much as a minute; then he raised up and sighed, and says, 'Confound it, I don't seem to understand this thing, no way; however, I'll tackle her again.' He fetched another acorn, and done his level best to see what become of it, but he couldn't. He says, 'Well, *I* never struck no such a hole as this before; I'm of the opinion it's a totally new kind of a hole.' Then he begun to get mad. He held in for a spell, walking up and down the comb of the roof and shaking his head and muttering to himself; but his feelings got the upper hand of him, presently, and he broke loose and cussed himself black in the face. I never see a bird take on so about a little thing. When he got through he walks to the hole and looks in again for half a minute; then he says, 'Well, you're a long hole, and a deep hole, and a mighty singular hole altogether—but I've started in to fill you, and I'm d—d if I *don't* fill you, if it takes a hundred years!'

"And with that, away he went. You never see a bird work so since you was born. He laid into his work like a nigger, and the way he hove acorns into that hole for about two hours and a half was one of the most exciting and astonishing spectacles I ever struck. He never stopped to take a look any more—he just hove 'em in and went for more. Well, at last he could hardly flop his wings, he was so tuckered out. He comes a-drooping down, once more, sweating like an ice-pitcher, drops his acorn in and says, '*Now* I guess I've got the bulge on you by this time!' So he bent down for a look. If you'll believe me, when his head come up again he was just pale with rage. He says, 'I've shoveled acorns enough in there to keep the family thirty years, and if I can see a sign of one of 'em I wish I may land in a museum with a belly full of sawdust in two minutes!'

"He just had strength enough to crawl up on to the comb and lean his back agin the chimbly, and then he collected his impressions and begun to free his mind. I see in a second that what I had mistook for profanity in the mines was only just the rudiments, as you may say.

"Another jay was going by, and heard him doing his devotions, and stops to inquire what was up. The sufferer told him the whole circumstance, and says, 'Now yonder's the hole, and if you don't believe me, go and look for yourself.' So this fellow went and looked, and comes back and says, 'How many did you say you put in there?' 'Not any less than two tons,' says the sufferer. The other jay went and looked again. He couldn't seem to make it out, so he raised a yell, and three more jays come. They all examined the hole, they all made the sufferer tell it over again, then they all discussed it, and got off as many leather-headed opinions about it as an average crowd of humans could have done.

"They called in more jays; then more and more, till pretty soon this whole region 'peared to have a blue flush about it. There must have been five thousand of them; and such another jawing and disputing and ripping and cussing, you never heard. Every jay in the whole lot put his eye to the hole and delivered a more chuckle-headed opinion about the mystery than the jay that went there before him. They examined the house all over, too. The door was standing half open, and at last one old jay happened to go and light on it and look in. Of course, that knocked the mystery galley-west in a second. There lay the acorns, scattered all over the floor. He flopped his wings and raised a whoop. 'Come here!' he says, 'Come here, everybody; hang'd if this fool hasn't been trying to fill up a house with acorns!' They all came a-swooping down like a blue cloud, and as each fellow lit on the door and took a glance, the whole absurdity of the contract that that first jay had tackled hit him home and he fell over backward suffocating with laughter, and the next jay took his place and done the same.

"Well, sir, they roosted around here on the housetop and the trees for an hour, and guffawed over that thing like human beings. It ain't any use to tell me a bluejay hasn't got a sense of humor, because I know better. And memory, too. They brought jays here from all over the United States to look down that hole, every summer for three years. Other birds, too. And they could all see the point, except an owl that come from Nova Scotia to visit the Yo Semite, and he took this thing in on his way back. He said he couldn't see anything funny in it. But then he was a good deal disappointed about Yo Semite, too."

CHAPTER IV

STUDENT LIFE

THE summer semester was in full tide; consequently the most frequent figure in and about Heidelberg was the student. Most of the students were Germans, of course, but the representatives of foreign lands were very numerous. They hailed from every corner of the globe—for instruction is cheap in Heidelberg, and so is living, too. The Anglo-American Club, composed of British and American students, had twenty-five members, and there was still much material left to draw from.

Nine-tenths of the Heidelberg students wore no badge or uniform; the other tenth wore caps of various colors, and belonged to social organizations called "corps." There were five corps, each with a color of its own; there were white caps, blue caps, and red, yellow, and green ones. The famous duel-fighting is confined to the "corps" boys. The "*kneip*" seems to be a specialty of theirs, too. Kneips are held, now and then, to celebrate great occasions, like the election of a beer king, for instance. The solemnity is simple; the five corps assemble at night, and at a signal they all fall loading themselves with beer, out of pint-mugs, as fast as possible, and each man keeps his own count—

23

usually by laying aside a lucifer match for each mug he empties. The election is soon decided. When the candidates can hold no more, a count is instituted and the one who has drank the greatest number of pints is proclaimed king. I was told that the last beer king elected by the corps—or by his own capabilities—emptied his mug seventy-five times. No stomach could hold all that quantity at one time, of course—but there are ways of frequently creating a vacuum, which those who have been much at sea will understand.

One sees so many students abroad at all hours, that he presently begins to wonder if they ever have any working-hours. Some of them have, some of them haven't. Each can choose for himself whether he will work or play; for German university life is a very free life; it seems to have no restraints. The student does not live in the college buildings, but hires his own lodgings, in any locality he prefers, and he takes his meals when and where he pleases. He goes to bed when it suits him, and does not get up at all unless he wants to. He is not entered at the university for any particular length of time; so he is likely to change about. He passes no examination upon entering college. He merely pays a trifling fee of five or ten dollars, receives a card entitling him to the privileges of the university, and that is the end of it. He is now ready for business —or play, as he shall prefer. If he elects to work, he finds a large list of lectures to choose from. He selects the subjects which he will study, and enters his name for these studies; but he can skip attendance.

The result of this system is, that lecture-courses upon specialties of an unusual nature are often delivered to very slim audiences, while those upon more practical and every-day matters of education are delivered to very large ones. I heard of one case where, day after day, the lecturer's audience consisted of three students—and always the same three. But one day two of them remained away. The lecturer began as usual—

"Gentlemen,"—

—then, without a smile, he corrected himself, saying—

"Sir,"—

—and went on with his discourse.

It is said that the vast majority of the Heidelberg students are hard workers, and make the most of their opportunities; that they have no surplus means to spend in dissipation, and no time to spare for frolicking. One lecture follows right on the heels of another, with very little time for the student to get out of one hall and into the next; but the industrious ones manage it by going on a trot. The professors assist them in the saving of their time by being promptly in their little boxed-up pulpits when the hours strike, and as promptly out again when the hour finishes. I entered an empty lecture-room one day just before the clock struck. The place had simple, unpainted pine desks and benches for about two hundred persons.

About a minute before the clock struck, a hundred and fifty students swarmed in, rushed to their seats, immediately spread open their note-books and dipped their pens in the ink. When the clock began to strike, a burly professor entered, was received with a round of applause, moved swiftly down the center aisle, said "Gentlemen," and began to talk as he climbed his pulpit steps; and by the time he had arrived in his box and faced his audience, his lecture was well under way and all the pens were going. He had no notes, he talked with prodigious rapidity and energy for an hour—then the students began to remind him in certain well-understood ways that his time was up; he seized his hat, still talking, proceeded swiftly down his pulpit steps, got out the last word of his discourse as he struck the floor; everybody rose respectfully, and he swept rapidly down the aisle and disappeared. An instant rush for some other lecture-room followed, and in a minute I was alone with the empty benches once more.

Yes, without doubt, idle students are not the rule. Out of eight hundred in the town, I knew the faces of only about fifty; but these I saw everywhere, and daily. They walked about the streets and the wooded hills, they drove in cabs, they boated on the river, they sipped beer and coffee, afternoons, in the Schloss gardens. A good many of them wore the colored caps of the corps. They were finely and fashionably dressed, their manners were quite superb, and they led an easy, careless, comfortable life. If a dozen of them sat together, and a lady or a gentleman passed whom one of them knew and saluted, they all rose to their feet and ook off their caps. The members of a corps always received a fellow-member in this way, too; but they paid no attention to members of other corps; they did not seem to see them. This was not a discourtesy; it was only a part of the elaborate and rigid corps etiquette.

There seems to be no chilly distance existing between the German students and the professor; but, on the contrary, a companionable intercourse, the opposite of chilliness and reserve. When the professor enters a beer-hall in the evening where students are gathered together, these rise up and take off their caps, and invite the old gentleman to sit with them and partake. He accepts, and the pleasant talk and the beer flow for an hour or two, and by and by the professor, properly charged and comfortable, gives a cordial good night, while the students stand bowing and uncovered; and then he moves on his happy way homeward with all his vast cargo of learning afloat in his hold. Nobody finds fault or feels outraged; no harm has been done.

It seemed to be a part of corps etiquette to keep a dog or so, too. I mean a corps dog—the common property of the organization, like the corps steward or head servant; then there are other dogs, owned by individuals.

On a summer afternoon in the Castle gardens, I have seen six students march solemnly into the grounds, in single file, each carrying a bright Chinese parasol and leading a prodigious dog by a string. It was a very imposing spectacle. Sometimes there would be about as many dogs around the pavilion as students; and of all breeds and of all degrees of beauty and ugliness. These dogs had a rather dry time of it; for they were tied to the benches and had no amusement for an hour or two at a time except what they could get out of pawing at the gnats, or trying to sleep and not succeeding. However, they got a lump of sugar occasionally—they were fond of that.

It seemed right and proper that students should indulge in dogs; but everybody else had them, too —old men and young ones, old women and nice young ladies. If there is one spectacle that is unpleasanter than another, it is that of an elegantly dressed young lady towing a dog by a string. It is said to be the sign and symbol of blighted love. It seems to me that some other way of advertising it might be devised, which would be just as conspicuous and yet not so trying to the proprieties.

It would be a mistake to suppose that the easy-going pleasure-seeking student carries an empty head. Just the contrary. He has spent nine years in the gymnasium, under a system which allowed him no freedom, but vigorously compelled him to work like a slave. Consequently, he has left the gymnasium with an education which is so extensive and complete, that the most a university can do for it is to perfect some of its profounder specialties. It is said that when a pupil leaves the gymnasium, he not only has a comprehensive education, but he *knows* what he knows—it is not befogged with uncertainty, it is burnt into him so that it will stay.

For instance, he does not merely read and write Greek, but speaks it; the same with the Latin. Foreign youth steer clear of the gymnasium; its rules are too severe. They go to the university to put a mansard roof on their whole general education; but the German student already has his mansard roof, so he goes there to add a steeple in the nature of some specialty, such as a particular branch of law, or medicine, or philology—like international law, or diseases of the eye, or special study of the ancient Gothic tongues. So this German attends only the lectures which belong to the chosen branch, and drinks his beer and tows his dog around and has a general good time the rest of the day. He has been in rigid bondage so long that the large liberty of university life is just what he needs and likes and thoroughly appreciates; and as it cannot last forever, he makes the most of it while it does last, and so lays up a good rest against the day that must see him put on the chains once more and enter the slavery of official or professional life.

CHAPTER V

AT THE STUDENTS' DUELING-GROUND

ONE day in the interest of science my agent obtained permission to bring me to the students' dueling-place. We crossed the river and drove up the bank a few hundred yards, then turned to the left, entered a narrow alley, followed it a hundred yards and arrived at a two-story public house; we were acquainted with its outside aspect, for it was visible from the hotel. We went up-stairs and passed into a large whitewashed apartment which was perhaps fifty feet long by thirty feet wide and twenty or twenty-five high. It was a well-lighted place. There was no carpet. Across one end and down both sides of the room extended a row of tables, and at these tables some fifty or seventy-five students [1] were sitting.

Some of them were sipping wine, others were playing cards, others chess, other groups were chatting together, and many were smoking cigarettes while they waited for the coming duels. Nearly all of them wore colored caps; there were white caps, green caps, blue caps, red caps, and bright-yellow ones; so, all the five corps were present in strong force. In the windows at the vacant end of the

[1] See Appendix C.

room stood six or eight long, narrow-bladed swords with large protecting guards for the hand, and outside was a man at work sharpening others on a grindstone. He understood his business; for when a sword left his hand one could shave himself with it.

It was observable that the young gentlemen neither bowed to nor spoke with students whose caps differed in color from their own. This did not mean hostility, but only an armed neutrality. It was considered that a person could strike harder in the duel, and with a more earnest interest, if he had never been in a condition of comradeship with his antagonist; therefore, comradeship between the corps was not permitted. At intervals the presidents of the five corps have a cold official intercourse with each other, but nothing further. For example, when the regular dueling-day of one of the corps approaches, its president calls for volunteers from among the membership to offer battle; three or more respond —but there must not be less than three; the president lays their names before the other presidents, with the request that they furnish antagonists for these challengers from among their corps. This is promptly done. It chanced that the present occasion was the battle-day of the Red Cap Corps. They were the challengers, and certain caps of other colors had volunteered to meet them. The students fight duels in the room which I have described, *two days in every week during seven and a half or eight months in every year.* This custom has continued in Germany two hundred and fifty years.

To return to my narrative. A student in a white

cap met us and introduced us to six or eight friends of his who also wore white caps, and while we stood conversing, two strange-looking figures were led in from another room. They were students panoplied for the duel. They were bareheaded; their eyes were protected by iron goggles which projected an inch or more, the leather straps of which bound their ears flat against their heads; their necks were wound around and around with thick wrappings which a sword could not cut through; from chin to ankle they were padded thoroughly against injury; their arms were bandaged and rebandaged, layer upon layer, until they looked like solid black logs. These weird apparitions had been handsome youths, clad in fashionable attire, fifteen minutes before, but now they did not resemble any beings one ever sees unless in nightmares. They strode along, with their arms projecting straight out from their bodies; they did not hold them out themselves, but fellow-students walked beside them and gave the needed support.

There was a rush for the vacant end of the room, now, and we followed and got good places. The combatants were placed face to face, each with several members of his own corps about him to assist; two seconds, well padded, and with swords in their hands, took near stations; a student belonging to neither of the opposing corps placed himself in a good position to umpire the combat; another student stood by with a watch and a memorandum-book to keep record of the time and the number and nature of the wounds; a gray-haired surgeon was present with his lint, his bandages, and his instruments. After a moment's pause the duelists saluted the umpire respectfully, then one after another the several officials stepped forward, gracefully removed their caps and saluted him also, and returned to their places. Everything was ready now; students stood crowded together in the foreground, and others stood behind them on chairs and tables. Every face was turned toward the center of attraction.

The combatants were watching each other with alert eyes; a perfect stillness, a breathless interest reigned. I felt that I was going to see some wary work. But not so. The instant the word was given, the two apparitions sprang forward and began to rain blows down upon each other with such lightning rapidity that I could not quite tell whether I saw the swords or only flashes they made in the air; the rattling din of these blows as they struck steel or paddings was something wonderfully stirring, and they were struck with such terrific force that I could not understand why the opposing sword was not beaten down under the assault. Presently, in the midst of the sword-flashes, I saw a handful of hair skip into the air as if it had lain loose on the victim's head and a breath of wind had puffed it suddenly away.

The seconds cried "Halt!" and knocked up the combatants' swords with their own. The duelists sat down; a student official stepped forward, examined the wounded head and touched the place with a sponge once or twice; the surgeon came and turned back the hair from the wound—and revealed a crimson gash two or three inches long, and proceeded to bind an oval piece of leather and a bunch of lint over it; the tally-keeper stepped up and tallied one for the opposition in his book.

Then the duelists took position again; a small stream of blood was flowing down the side of the injured man's head, and over his shoulder and down his body to the floor, but he did not seem to mind this. The word was given, and they plunged at each other as fiercely as before; once more the blows rained and rattled and flashed; every few moments the quick-eyed seconds would notice that a sword was bent—then they called "Halt!" struck up the contending weapons, and an assisting student straightened the bent one.

The wonderful turmoil went on—presently a bright spark sprung from a blade, and that blade, broken in several pieces, sent one of its fragments flying to the ceiling. A new sword was provided, and the fight proceeded. The exercise was tremendous, of course, and in time the fighters began to show great fatigue. They were allowed to rest a moment, every little while; they got other rests by wounding each other, for then they could sit down while the doctor applied the lint and bandages. The law is that the battle must continue fifteen minutes if the men can hold out; and as the pauses do not count, this duel was protracted to twenty or thirty minutes, I judged. At last it was decided that the men were too much wearied to do battle longer. They were led away drenched with crimson from head to foot. That was a good fight, but it could not count, partly because it did not last the lawful fifteen minutes (of actual fighting), and partly because neither man was disabled by his wounds. It was a drawn battle, and corps law requires that drawn battles shall be refought as soon as the adversaries are well of their hurts.

During the conflict, I had talked a little, now and then, with a young gentleman of the White Cap Corps, and he had mentioned that he was to fight next—and had also pointed out his challenger, a young gentleman who was leaning against the opposite wall smoking a cigarette and restfully observing the duel then in progress.

My acquaintanceship with a party to the coming contest had the effect of giving me a kind of personal interest in it; I naturally wished he might win, and it was the reverse of pleasant to learn that he probably would not, because, although he was a notable swordsman, the challenger was held to be his superior.

The duel presently began and in the same furious way which had marked the previous one. I stood close by, but could not tell which blows told and which did not, they fell and vanished so like flashes of light. They all seemed to tell; the swords always bent over the opponents' heads, from the forehead back over the crown, and seemed to touch, all the way; but it was not so—a protecting blade, invisible to me, was always interposed between. At the end of ten seconds each man had struck twelve or fifteen blows, and warded off twelve or fifteen, and no harm done; then a sword became disabled, and a short rest followed whilst a new one was brought. Early in the next round the White Corps student got an ugly wound on the side of his head and gave his opponent one like it. In the third round the latter received another bad wound in the head, and the former had his under-lip divided. After that, the White Corps student gave many severe wounds, but got none of consequence in return. At the end of five minutes from the beginning of the duel the surgeon stopped it; the challenging party had suffered such injuries that any addition to them might be dangerous. These injuries were a fearful spectacle, but are better left undescribed. So, against expectation, my acquaintance was the victor.

CHAPTER VI

THE third duel was brief and bloody. The surgeon stopped it when he saw that one of the men had received such bad wounds that he could not fight longer without endangering his life.

The fourth duel was a tremendous encounter; but at the end of five or six minutes the surgeon interfered once more: another man so severely hurt as to render it unsafe to add to his harms. I watched this engagement as I had watched the others—with rapt interest and strong excitement, and with a shrink and a shudder for every blow that laid open a cheek or a forehead; and a conscious paling of my face when I occasionally saw a wound of a yet more shocking nature inflicted. My eyes were upon the loser of this duel when he got his last and vanquishing wound—it was in his face and it carried away his —but no matter, I must not enter into details. I had but a glance, and then turned quickly away, but I would not have been looking at all if I had known what was coming. No, that is probably not true; one thinks he would not look if he knew what was coming, but the interest and the excitement are so powerful that they would doubtless conquer all other feelings; and so, under the fierce exhilaration of the clashing steel, he would yield and look, after all.

Sometimes spectators of these duels faint—and it does seem a very reasonable thing to do, too.

Both parties to this fourth duel were badly hurt; so much so that the surgeon was at work upon them nearly or quite an hour—a fact which is suggestive. But this waiting interval was not wasted in idleness by the assembled students. It was past noon; therefore they ordered their landlord, down-stairs, to send up hot beefsteaks, chickens, and such things, and these they ate, sitting comfortably at the several tables, whilst they chatted, disputed and laughed. The door to the surgeon's room stood open, mean-time, but the cutting, sewing, splicing, and bandaging going on in there in plain view did not seem to dis-turb any one's appetite. I went in and saw the sur-geon labor awhile, but could not enjoy it; it was much less trying to see the wounds given and re-ceived than to see them mended; the stir and tur-moil, and the music of the steel, were wanting here —one's nerves were wrung by this grisly spectacle, whilst the duel's compensating pleasurable thrill was lacking.

Finally the doctor finished, and the men who were to fight the closing battle of the day came forth. A good many dinners were not completed, yet, but no matter, they could be eaten cold, after the battle; therefore everybody crowded forward to see. This was not a love duel, but a "satisfaction" affair. These two students had quarreled, and were here to settle it. They did not belong to any of the corps, but they were furnished with weapons and armor, and permitted to fight here by the five corps as a

THE DELUGE OF BLOWS BEGAN

courtesy. Evidently these two young men were
unfamiliar with the dueling ceremonies, though they
were not unfamiliar with the sword. When they
were placed in position they thought it was time to
begin—and they did begin, too, and with a most
impetuous energy, without waiting for anybody to
give the word. This vastly amused the spectators,
and even broke down their studied and courtly
gravity and surprised them into laughter. Of course
the seconds struck up the swords and started the
duel over again. At the word, the deluge of blows
began, but before long the surgeon once more interfered—for the only reason which ever permits him
to interfere—and the day's war was over. It was
now two in the afternoon, and I had been present
since half past nine in the morning. The field of
battle was indeed a red one by this time; but some
sawdust soon righted that. There had been one
duel before I arrived. In it one of the men received
many injuries, while the other one escaped without
a scratch.

I had seen the heads and faces of ten youths
gashed in every direction by the keen two-edged
blades, and yet had not seen a victim wince, nor
heard a moan, or detected any fleeting expression
which confessed the sharp pain the hurts were inflict-
ing. This was good fortitude, indeed. Such endur-
ance is to be expected in savages and prize-fighters,
for they are born and educated to it; but to find it
in such perfection in these gently bred and kindly
natured young fellows is matter for surprise. It was
not merely under the excitement of the sword-play

that this fortitude was shown; it was shown in the surgeon's room where an uninspiring quiet reigned, and where there was no audience. The doctor's manipulations brought out neither grimaces nor moans. And in the fights it was observable that these lads hacked and slashed with the same tremendous spirit, after they were covered with streaming wounds, which they had shown in the beginning.

The world in general looks upon the college duels as very farcical affairs: true, but considering that the college duel is fought by boys; that the swords are real swords; and that the head and face are exposed, it seems to me that it is a farce which has quite a grave side to it. People laugh at it mainly because they think the student is so covered up with armor that he cannot be hurt. But it is not so; his eyes and ears are protected, but the rest of his face and head are bare. He can not only be badly wounded, but his life is in danger; and he would sometimes lose it but for the interference of the surgeon. It is not intended that his life shall be endangered. Fatal accidents are possible, however. For instance, the student's sword may break, and the end of it fly up behind his antagonist's ear and cut an artery which could not be reached if the sword remained whole. This has happened, sometimes, and death has resulted on the spot. Formerly the student's armpits were not protected—and at that time the swords were pointed, whereas they are blunt, now; so an artery in the armpit was sometimes cut, and death followed. Then in the days of sharp-pointed swords, a spectator was an occasional victim—the end of a

broken sword flew five or ten feet and buried itself
in his neck or his heart, and death ensued instantly.
The student duels in Germany occasion two or three
deaths every year, now, but this arises only from the
carelessness of the wounded men; they eat or drink
imprudently, or commit excesses in the way of over-
exertion; inflammation sets in and gets such a head-
way that it cannot be arrested. Indeed, there is
blood and pain and danger enough about the college
duel to entitle it to a considerable degree of respect.

All the customs, all the laws, all the details, per-
taining to the student duel are quaint and naïve.
The grave, precise, and courtly ceremony with which
the thing is conducted, invests it with a sort of
antique charm.

This dignity and these knightly graces suggest the
tournament, not the prize-fight. The laws are as
curious as they are strict. For instance, the duelist
may step forward from the line he is placed upon,
if he chooses, but never back of it. If he steps back
of it, or even leans back, it is considered that he did
it to avoid a blow or contrive an advantage; so he
is dismissed from his corps in disgrace. It would
seem but natural to step from under a descending
sword unconsciously, and against one's will and
intent — yet this unconsciousness is not allowed.
Again: if under the sudden anguish of a wound the
receiver of it makes a grimace, he falls some degrees
in the estimation of his fellows; his corps are
ashamed of him: they call him "hare foot," which
is the German equivalent for chicken-hearted.

CHAPTER VII

IN addition to the corps laws, there are some corps usages which have the force of laws.

Perhaps the president of a corps notices that one of the membership who is no longer an exempt—that is a freshman—has remained a sophomore some little time without volunteering to fight; some day, the president, instead of calling for volunteers, will *appoint* this sophomore to measure swords with a student of another corps; he is free to decline—everybody says so—there is no compulsion. This is all true—but I have not heard of any student who *did* decline. He would naturally rather retire from the corps than decline; to decline and still remain in the corps would make him unpleasantly conspicuous, and properly so, since he knew, when he joined, that his main business, as a member, would be to fight. No, there is no law against declining —except the law of custom, which is confessedly stronger than written law, everywhere.

The ten men whose duels I had witnessed did not go away when their hurts were dressed, as I had supposed they would, but came back, one after another, as soon as they were free of the surgeon, and mingled with the assemblage in the dueling-room. The white-cap student who won the second fight witnessed the remaining three, and talked with us during the intermissions. He could not talk very well, because his opponent's sword had cut his under-lip in two, and then the surgeon had sewed it together and overlaid it with a profusion of white plaster patches; neither could he eat easily, still he contrived to accomplish a slow and troublesome luncheon while the last duel was preparing. The man who was the worst hurt of all played chess while waiting to see this engagement. A good part of his face was covered with patches and bandages, and all the rest of his head was covered and concealed by them. It is said that the student likes to appear on the street and in other public places in this kind of array, and that this predilection often keeps him out when exposure to rain or sun is a positive danger for him. Newly bandaged students are a very common spectacle in the public gardens of Heidelberg. It is also said that the student is glad to get wounds in the face, because the scars they leave will show so well there; and it is also said that these face wounds are so prized that youths have even been known to pull them apart from time to time and put red wine in them to make them heal badly and leave as ugly a scar as possible. It does not look reasonable, but it is roundly asserted and maintained, nevertheless; I am sure of one thing—scars are plenty enough in Germany, among the young men; and very grim ones they are, too. They crisscross the face in angry red welts, and are permanent and ineffaceable. Some of these scars are of a very strange and dreadful aspect; and the effect is striking when several such accent the milder ones, which form a city map on a man's face; they suggest the "burned district" then. We had often noticed that many of the students wore a colored silk band or ribbon diagonally across their breasts. It transpired that this signifies that the wearer has fought three duels in which a decision was reached —duels in which he either whipped or was whipped —for drawn battles do not count.[1] After a student has received his ribbon, he is "free"; he can cease from fighting, without reproach—except some one insult him; his president cannot appoint him to fight; he can volunteer if he wants to, or remain quiescent if he prefers to do so. Statistics show that he does *not* prefer to remain quiescent. They show that the duel has a singular fascination about it somewhere, for these free men, so far from resting upon the privilege of the badge, are always volunteering. A corps student told me it was of record that Prince Bismarck fought thirty-two of these duels in a single summer term when he was in college. So he fought twenty-nine after his badge had given him the right to retire from the field.

The statistics may be found to possess interest in several particulars. Two days in every week are devoted to dueling. The rule is rigid that there

[1] FROM MY DIARY.—Dined in a hotel a few miles up the Neckar, in a room whose walls were hung all over with framed portrait-groups of the Five Corps; some were recent, but many antedated photography, and were pictured in lithography—the dates ranged back to forty or fifty years ago. Nearly every individual wore the ribbon across his breast. In one portrait-group representing (as each of these pictures did) an entire Corps, I took pains to count the ribbons: there were twenty-seven members, and twenty-one of them wore that significant badge.

must be three duels on each of these days; there are generally more, but there cannot be fewer. There were six the day I was present; sometimes there are seven or eight. It is insisted that eight duels a week—four for each of the two days—is too low an average to draw a calculation from, but I will reckon from that basis, preferring an understatement to an overstatement of the case. This requires about four hundred and eighty or five hundred duelists in a year—for in summer the college term is about three and a half months, and in winter it is four months and sometimes longer. Of the seven hundred and fifty students in the university at the time I am writing of, only eighty belonged to the five corps, and it is only these corps that do the dueling; occasionally other students borrow the arms and battleground of the five corps in order to settle a quarrel, but this does not happen every dueling-day.[1] Consequently eighty youths furnish the material for some two hundred and fifty duels a year. This average gives six fights a year to each of the eighty. This large work could not be accomplished if the badge-holders stood upon their privilege and ceased to volunteer.

Of course, where there is so much fighting, the students make it a point to keep themselves in constant practice with the foil. One often sees them, at the tables in the Castle grounds, using their whips or canes to illustrate some new sword trick which they

---

[1] They have to borrow the arms because they could not get them elsewhere or otherwise. As I understand it, the public authorities, all over Germany, allow the five Corps to keep swords, but *do not allow them to use them.* This law is rigid; it is only the execution of it that is lax.

have heard about; and between the duels, on the day whose history I have been writing, the swords were not always idle; every now and then we heard a

succession of the keen hissing sounds which the sword makes when it is being put through its paces in the air, and this informed us that a student was practising. Necessarily, this unceasing attention to the art develops an expert occasionally. He becomes famous in his own university, his renown spreads to other universities. He is invited to Göttingen, to fight with a Göttingen expert; if he is victorious, he will be invited to other colleges, or those colleges will send their experts to him. Americans and Englishmen often join one or another of the five corps. A year or two ago, the principal Heidelberg expert was a big Kentuckian; he was invited to the various universities and left a wake of victory behind him all about Germany; but at last a little student in Strasburg defeated him. There was formerly a student in Heidelberg who had picked up somewhere and mastered a peculiar trick of cutting

PIECE OF SWORD

up under instead of cleaving down from above. While the trick lasted he won in sixteen successive duels in his own university; but by that time observers had discovered what his charm was, and how to break it, therefore his championship ceased.

46

The rule which forbids social intercourse between members of different corps is strict. In the dueling-house, in the parks, on the street, and anywhere and everywhere that students go, caps of a color group themselves together. If all the tables in a public garden were crowded but one, and that one had two red-cap students at it and ten vacant places, the yellow caps, the blue caps, the white caps, and the green caps, seeking seats, would go by that table and not seem to see it, nor seem to be aware that there was such a table in the grounds. The student by whose courtesy we had been enabled to visit the dueling-place, wore the white cap—Prussian Corps. He introduced us to many white caps, but to none of another color. The corps etiquette extended even to us, who were strangers, and required us to group with the white corps only, and speak only with the white corps, while we were their guests, and keep aloof from caps of the other colors. Once I wished to examine some of the swords, but an American student said, "It would not be quite polite; these now in the windows all have red hilts or blue; they will bring in some with white hilts presently, and those you can handle freely." When a sword was broken in the first duel, I wanted a piece of it; but its hilt was the wrong color, so it was considered best and politest to await a properer season. It was brought to me after the room was cleared, and I will now make a "life-size" sketch of it by tracing a line around it with my pen, to show the width of the weapon. The length of these swords is about three feet, and they are quite heavy. One's disposition to cheer, during the course of the duels or at their close, was naturally strong, but corps etiquette forbade any demonstrations of this sort. However brilliant a contest or a victory might be, no sign or sound betrayed that any one was moved. A dignified gravity and repression were maintained at all times.

When the dueling was finished and we were ready to go, the gentlemen of the Prussian Corps to whom we had been introduced took off their caps in the courteous German way, and also shook hands; their brethren of the same order took off their caps and bowed, but without shaking hands; the gentlemen of the other corps treated us just as they would have treated white caps—they fell apart, apparently unconsciously, and left us an unobstructed pathway, but did not seem to see us or know we were there. If we had gone thither the following week as guests of another corps, the white caps, without meaning any offense, would have observed the etiquette of their order and ignored our presence.

[How strangely are comedy and tragedy blended in this life! I had not been home a full half-hour, after witnessing those playful sham-duels, when circumstances made it necessary for me to get ready immediately to assist personally at a real one—a duel with no effeminate limitations in the matter of results, but a battle to the death. An account of it, in the next chapter, will show the reader that duels between boys, for fun, and duels between men in earnest, are very different affairs.]

CHAPTER VIII

MUCH as the modern French duel is ridiculed by
certain smart people, it is in reality one of the
most dangerous institutions of our day. Since it is
always fought in the open air, the combatants are
nearly sure to catch cold. M. Paul de Cassagnac,
the most inveterate of the French duelists, had
suffered so often in this way that he is at last a confirmed invalid; and the best physician in Paris has
expressed the opinion that if he goes on dueling for
fifteen or twenty years more—unless he forms the
habit of fighting in a comfortable room where damps
and draughts cannot intrude—he will eventually
endanger his life. This ought to moderate the talk
of those people who are so stubborn in maintaining
that the French duel is the most health-giving of
recreations because of the open-air exercise it affords.
And it ought also to moderate that foolish talk about
French duelists and socialist-hated monarchs being
the only people who are immortal.

But it is time to get at my subject. As soon as I
heard of the late fiery outbreak between M. Gambetta and M. Fourtou in the French Assembly, I
knew that trouble must follow. I knew it because
a long personal friendship with M. Gambetta had

revealed to me the desperate and implacable nature of the man. Vast as are his physical proportions, I knew that the thirst for revenge would penetrate to the remotest frontiers of his person.

I did not wait for him to call on me, but went at once to him. As I had expected, I found the brave fellow steeped in a profound French calm. I say French calm, because French calmness and English calmness have points of difference. He was moving swiftly back and forth among the debris of his furniture, now and then staving chance fragments of it across the room with his foot; grinding a constant grist of curses through his set teeth; and halting every little while to deposit another handful of his hair on the pile which he had been building of it on the table.

He threw his arms around my neck, bent me over his stomach to his breast, kissed me on both cheeks, hugged me four or five times, and then placed me in his own arm-chair. As soon as I had got well again, we began business at once.

I said I supposed he would wish me to act as his second, and he said, "Of course." I said I must be allowed to act under a French name, so that I might be shielded from obloquy in my country, in case of fatal results. He winced here, probably at the suggestion that dueling was not regarded with respect in America. However, he agreed to my requirement. This accounts for the fact that in all the newspaper reports M. Gambetta's second was apparently a Frenchman.

First, we drew up my principal's will. I insisted

upon this, and stuck to my point. I said I had never heard of a man in his right mind going out to fight a duel without first making his will. He said he had never heard of a man in his right mind doing anything of the kind. When he had finished the will, he wished to proceed to a choice of his "last words." He wanted to know how the following words, as a dying exclamation, struck me:

"I die for my God, for my country, for freedom of speech, for progress, and the universal brotherhood of man!"

I objected that this would require too lingering a death; it was a good speech for a consumptive, but not suited to the exigencies of the field of honor. We wrangled over a good many ante-mortem outbursts, but I finally got him to cut his obituary down to this, which he copied into his memorandum-book, purposing to get it by heart:

"I DIE THAT FRANCE MAY LIVE."

I said that this remark seemed to lack relevancy; but he said relevancy was a matter of no consequence in last words, what you wanted was thrill.

The next thing in order was the choice of weapons. My principal said he was not feeling well, and would leave that and the other details of the proposed meeting to me. Therefore I wrote the following note and carried it to M. Fourtou's friend:

SIR: M. Gambetta accepts M. Fourtou's challenge, and authorizes me to propose Plessis-Piquet as the place of meeting; to-morrow morning at daybreak as the time; and axes as the weapons. I am, sir, with great respect,

MARK TWAIN.

M. Fourtou's friend read this note, and shuddered. Then he turned to me, and said, with a suggestion of severity in his tone:

"Have you considered, sir, what would be the inevitable result of such a meeting as this?"

"Well, for instance, what *would* it be?"

"Bloodshed!"

"That's about the size of it," I said. "Now, if it is a fair question, what was your side proposing to shed?"

I had him there. He saw he had made a blunder, so he hastened to explain it away. He said he had spoken jestingly. Then he added that he and his principal would enjoy axes, and indeed prefer them, but such weapons were barred by the French code, and so I must change my proposal.

I walked the floor, turning the thing over in my mind, and finally it occurred to me that Gatling-guns at fifteen paces would be a likely way to get a verdict on the field of honor. So I framed this idea into a proposition.

But it was not accepted. The code was in the way again. I proposed rifles; then double-barreled shotguns; then Colt's navy revolvers. These being all rejected, I reflected awhile, and sarcastically suggested brickbats at three-quarters of a mile. I always hate to fool away a humorous thing on a person who has no perception of humor; and it filled me with bitterness when this man went soberly away to submit the last proposition to his principal.

He came back presently and said his principal was charmed with the idea of brickbats at three-quarters of a mile, but must decline on account of the danger to disinterested parties passing between. Then I said:

"Well, I am at the end of my string, now. Perhaps *you* would be good enough to suggest a weapon? Perhaps you have even had one in your mind all the time?"

His countenance brightened, and he said with alacrity:

"Oh, without doubt, monsieur!"

So he fell to hunting in his pockets—pocket after pocket, and he had plenty of them—muttering all the while, "Now, what could I have done with them?"

At last he was successful. He fished out of his vest pocket a couple of little things which I carried to the light and ascertained to be pistols. They were single-barreled and silver-mounted, and very dainty and pretty. I was not able to speak for emotion. I silently hung one of them on my watch-chain, and returned the other. My companion in crime now unrolled a postage-stamp containing several cartridges, and gave me one of them. I asked if he meant to signify by this that our men were to be allowed but one shot apiece. He replied that the French code permitted no more. I then begged him to go on and suggest a distance, for my mind was growing weak and confused under the strain which had been put upon it. He named sixty-five yards. I nearly lost my patience. I said:

"Sixty - five yards, with these instruments? Squirt-guns would be deadlier at fifty. Consider, my friend, you and I are banded together to destroy life, not make it eternal."

But with all my persuasions, all my arguments, I was only able to get him to reduce the distance to thirty-five yards; and even this concession he made with reluctance, and said with a sigh, "I wash my hands of this slaughter; on your head be it."

There was nothing for me but to go home to my old lion-heart and tell my humiliating story. When I entered, M. Gambetta was laying his last lock of hair upon the altar. He sprang toward me, exclaiming:

"You have made the fatal arrangements—I see it in your eye!"

"I have."

His face paled a trifle, and he leaned upon the table for support. He breathed thick and heavily for a moment or two, so tumultuous were his feelings; then he hoarsely whispered:

"The weapon, the weapon! Quick! what is the weapon?"

"This!" and I displayed that silver-mounted thing. He cast but one glance at it, then swooned ponderously to the floor.

When he came to, he said mournfully:

"The unnatural calm to which I have subjected myself has told upon my nerves. But away with weakness! I will confront my fate like a man and a Frenchman."

He rose to his feet, and assumed an attitude which for sublimity has never been approached by man, and has seldom been surpassed by statues. Then he said, in his deep bass tones:

"Behold, I am calm, I am ready; reveal to me the distance."

"Thirty-five yards." . . .

I could not lift him up, of course; but I rolled him over, and poured water down his back. He presently came to, and said:

"Thirty-five yards—without a rest? But why ask? Since murder was that man's intention, why should he palter with small details? But mark you one thing: in my fall the world shall see how the chivalry of France meets death."

After a long silence he asked:

"Was nothing said about that man's family standing up with him, as an offset to my bulk? But no matter; I would not stoop to make such a suggestion; if he is not noble enough to suggest it himself, he is welcome to this advantage, which no honorable man would take."

He now sank into a sort of stupor of reflection, which lasted some minutes; after which he broke silence with:

"The hour—what is the hour fixed for the collision?"

"Dawn, to-morrow."

He seemed greatly surprised, and immediately said:

"Insanity! I never heard of such a thing. Nobody is abroad at such an hour."

"That is the reason I named it. Do you mean to say you want an audience?"

"It is no time to bandy words. I am astonished that M. Fourtou should ever have agreed to so strange an innovation. Go at once and require a later hour."

I ran down-stairs, threw open the front door, and almost plunged into the arms of M. Fourtou's second. He said:

"I have the honor to say that my principal strenuously objects to the hour chosen, and begs you will consent to change it to half past nine."

"Any courtesy, sir, which it is in our power to extend is at the service of your excellent principal. We agree to the proposed change of time."

"I beg you to accept the thanks of my client." Then he turned to a person behind him, and said, "You hear, M. Noir, the hour is altered to half past nine." Whereupon M. Noir bowed, expressed his thanks, and went away. My accomplice continued:

"If agreeable to you, your chief surgeons and ours shall proceed to the field in the same carriage, as is customary."

"It is entirely agreeable to me, and I am obliged to you for mentioning the surgeons, for I am afraid I should not have thought of them. How many shall I want? I suppose two or three will be enough?"

"Two is the customary number for each party. I refer to 'chief' surgeons; but considering the exalted positions occupied by our clients, it will be well and decorous that each of us appoint several consulting surgeons, from among the highest in the profession. These will come in their own private carriages. Have you engaged a hearse?"

"Bless my stupidity, I never thought of it! I

will attend to it right away. I must seem very ignorant to you; but you must try to overlook that, because I have never had any experience of such a swell duel as this before. I have had a good deal to do with duels on the Pacific coast, but I see now that they were crude affairs. A hearse—sho! we used to leave the elected lying around loose, and let anybody cord them up and cart them off that wanted to. Have you anything further to suggest?"

"Nothing, except that the head undertakers shall ride together, as is usual. The subordinates and mutes will go on foot, as is also usual. I will see you at eight o'clock in the morning, and we will then arrange the order of the procession. I have the honor to bid you a good day."

I returned to my client, who said, "Very well; at what hour is the engagement to begin?"

"Half past nine."

"Very good indeed. Have you sent the fact to the newspapers?"

"*Sir!* If after our long and intimate friendship you can for a moment deem me capable of so base a treachery—"

"Tut, tut! What words are these, my dear friend? Have I wounded you? Ah, forgive me; I am overloading you with labor. Therefore go on with the other details, and drop this one from your list. The bloody-minded Fourtou will be sure to attend to it. Or I myself—yes, to make certain, I will drop a note to my journalistic friend, M. Noir—"

"Oh, come to think of it, you may save yourself the trouble; that other second has informed M. Noir."

"H'm! I might have known it. It is just like that Fourtou, who always wants to make a display."

At half past nine in the morning, the procession approached the field of Plessis-Piquet in the following order: first came our carriage—nobody in it but M. Gambetta and myself; then a carriage containing M. Fourtou and his second; then a carriage containing two poet-orators who did not believe in God, and these had MS. funeral orations projecting from their breast pockets; then a carriage containing the head surgeons and their cases of instruments; then eight private carriages containing consulting surgeons; then a hack containing a coroner; then the two hearses; then a carriage containing the head undertakers; then a train of assistants and mutes on foot; and after these came plodding through the fog a long procession of camp followers, police, and citizens generally. It was a noble turnout, and would have made a fine display if we had had thinner weather.

There was no conversation. I spoke several times to my principal, but I judge he was not aware of it, for he always referred to his note-book and muttered absently, "I die that France may live."

Arrived on the field, my fellow-second and I paced off the thirty-five yards, and then drew lots for choice of position. This latter was but an ornamental ceremony, for all the choices were alike in such weather. These preliminaries being ended, I went to my principal and asked him if he was ready. He spread himself out to his full width, and said in a stern voice, "Ready! Let the batteries be charged."

The loading was done in the presence of duly constituted witnesses. We considered it best to perform this delicate service with the assistance of a lantern, on account of the state of the weather. We now placed our men.

At this point the police noticed that the public had massed themselves together on the right and left of the field; they therefore begged a delay, while they should put these poor people in a place of safety.

The request was granted.

The police having ordered the two multitudes to take positions behind the duelists, we were once more ready. The weather growing still more opaque, it was agreed between myself and the other second that before giving the fatal signal we should each deliver a loud whoop to enable the combatants to ascertain each other's whereabouts.

I now returned to my principal, and was distressed to observe that he had lost a good deal of his spirit. I tried my best to hearten him. I said, "Indeed, sir, things are not as bad as they seem. Considering the character of the weapons, the limited number of shots allowed, the generous distance, the impenetrable solidity of the fog, and the added fact that one of the combatants is one-eyed and the other cross-eyed and near-sighted, it seems to me that this conflict need not necessarily be fatal. There are chances that both of you may survive. Therefore, cheer up; do not be downhearted."

This speech had so good an effect that my principal immediately stretched forth his hand and said, "I am myself again; give me the weapon."

I laid it, all lonely and forlorn, in the center of the vast solitude of his palm. He gazed at it and shuddered. And still mournfully contemplating it, he murmured, in a broken voice:

"Alas, it is not death I dread, but mutilation."

I heartened him once more, and with such success that he presently said, "Let the tragedy begin. Stand at my back; do not desert me in this solemn hour, my friend."

I gave him my promise. I now assisted him to point his pistol toward the spot where I judged his adversary to be standing, and cautioned him to listen well and further guide himself by my fellow-second's whoop. Then I propped myself against M. Gambetta's back, and raised a rousing "Whoop-ee!" This was answered from out the far distances of the fog, and I immediately shouted:

"One—two—three—*fire!*"

Two little sounds like *spit! spit!* broke upon my ear, and in the same instant I was crushed to the earth under a mountain of flesh. Bruised as I was, I was still able to catch a faint accent from above, to this effect:

"I die for . . . for . . . perdition take it, what *is* it I die for? . . . oh, yes—FRANCE! I die that France may live!"

The surgeons swarmed around with their probes in their hands, and applied their microscopes to the whole area of M. Gambetta's person, with the happy result of finding nothing in the nature of a wound. Then a scene ensued which was in every way gratifying and inspiriting.

The two gladiators fell upon each other's neck, with floods of proud and happy tears; that other second embraced me; the surgeons, the orators, the undertakers, the police, everybody embraced, everybody congratulated, everybody cried, and the whole atmosphere was filled with praise and with joy unspeakable.

It seemed to me then that I would rather be a hero of a French duel than a crowned and sceptered monarch.

When the commotion had somewhat subsided, the body of surgeons held a consultation, and after a good deal of debate decided that with proper care and nursing there was reason to believe that I would survive my injuries. My internal hurts were deemed the most serious, since it was apparent that a broken rib had penetrated my left lung, and that many of my organs had been pressed out so far to one side or the other of where they belonged, that it was doubtful if they would ever learn to perform their functions in such remote and unaccustomed localities. They then set my left arm in two places, pulled my right hip into its socket again, and re-elevated my nose. I was an object of great interest, and even admiration; and many sincere and warm-hearted persons had themselves introduced to me, and said they were proud to know the only man who had been hurt in a French duel in forty years.

I was placed in an ambulance at the very head of the procession; and thus with gratifying *éclat* I was marched into Paris, the most conspicuous figure in that great spectacle, and deposited at the hospital.

The cross of the Legion of Honor has been conferred upon me. However, few escape that distinction.

Such is the true version of the most memorable private conflict of the age.

I have no complaints to make against any one. I acted for myself, and I can stand the consequences.

Without boasting, I think I may say I am not afraid to stand before a modern French duelist, but as long as I keep in my right mind I will never consent to stand behind one again.

CHAPTER IX

ONE day we took the train and went down to Mannheim to see "King Lear" played in German. It was a mistake. We sat in our seats three whole hours and never understood anything but the thunder and lightning; and even that was reversed to suit German ideas, for the thunder came first and the lightning followed after.

The behavior of the audience was perfect. There were no rustlings, or whisperings, or other little disturbances; each act was listened to in silence, and the applauding was done after the curtain was down. The doors opened at half past four, the play began promptly at half past five, and within two minutes afterward all who were coming were in their seats, and quiet reigned. A German gentleman in the train had said that a Shakespearian play was an appreciated treat in Germany and that we should find the house filled. It was true; all the six tiers were filled, and remained so to the end—which suggested that it is not only balcony people who like Shakespeare in Germany, but those of the pit and the gallery, too.

Another time, we went to Mannheim and attended a shivaree—otherwise an opera—the one called "Lohengrin." The banging and slamming and booming and crashing were something beyond belief. The racking and pitiless pain of it remains stored up in my memory alongside the memory of the time that I had my teeth fixed. There were circumstances which made it necessary for me to stay through the four hours to the end, and I stayed; but the recollection of that long, dragging, relentless season of suffering is indestructible. To have to endure it in silence, and sitting still, made it all the harder. I was in a railed compartment with eight or ten strangers, of the two sexes, and this compelled repression; yet at times the pain was so exquisite that I could hardly keep the tears back. At those times, as the howlings and wailings and shriekings of the singers, and the ragings and roarings and explosions of the vast orchestra rose higher and higher, and wilder and wilder, and fiercer and fiercer, I could have cried if I had been alone. Those strangers would not have been surprised to see a man do such a thing who was being gradually skinned, but they would have marveled at it here, and made remarks about it no doubt, whereas there was nothing in the present case which was an advantage over being skinned. There was a wait of half an hour at the end of the first act, and I could have gone out and rested during that time, but I could not trust myself to do it, for I felt that I should desert and stay out. There was another wait of half an hour toward nine o'clock, but I had gone through so much by that time that I had no spirit left, and so had no desire but to be let alone.

I do not wish to suggest that the rest of the peo-

A TRAMP ABROAD

ple there were like me, for, indeed, they were not.
Whether it was that they naturally liked that noise,
or whether it was that they had learned to like it by
getting used to it, I did not at that time know; but
they did like it—this was plain enough. While it
was going on they sat and looked as rapt and grateful as cats do when one strokes their backs; and
whenever the curtain fell they rose to their feet, in
one solid mighty multitude, and the air was snowed
thick with waving handkerchiefs, and hurricanes of
applause swept the place. This was not compre-
hensible to me. Of course, there were many people
there who were not under compulsion to stay; yet
the tiers were as full at the close as they had been
at the beginning. This showed that the people
liked it.

It was a curious sort of a play. In the matter of
costumes and scenery it was fine and showy enough;
but there was not much action. That is to say,
there was not much really done, it was only talked
about; and always violently. It was what one
might call a narrative play. Everybody had a
narrative and a grievance, and none were reasonable
about it, but all in an offensive and ungovernable
state. There was little of that sort of customary
thing where the tenor and the soprano stand down
by the footlights, warbling, with blended voices, and
keep holding out their arms toward each other and
drawing them back and spreading both hands over
first one breast and then the other with a shake and
a pressure—no, it was every rioter for himself and
no blending. Each sang his indictive narrative in

65

turn, accompanied by the whole orchestra of sixty
instruments, and when this had continued for some
time, and one was hoping they might come to an
understanding and modify the noise, a great chorus
composed entirely of maniacs would suddenly break
forth, and then during two minutes, and sometimes
three, I lived over again all that I had suffered the
time the orphan asylum burned down.

We only had one brief little season of heaven and
heaven's sweet ecstasy and peace during all this long
and diligent and acrimonious reproduction of the
other place. This was while a gorgeous procession
of people marched around and around, in the third
act, and sang the Wedding Chorus. To my un-
tutored ear that was music—almost divine music.
While my seared soul was steeped in the healing
balm of those gracious sounds, it seemed to me that
I could almost resuffer the torments which had
gone before, in order to be so healed again. There
is where the deep ingenuity of the operatic idea is
betrayed. It deals so largely in pain that its scattered delights are prodigiously augmented by the
contrasts. A pretty air in an opera is prettier there
than it could be anywhere else, I suppose, just as
an honest man in politics shines more than he would
elsewhere.

I have since found out that there is nothing the
Germans like so much as an opera. They like it,
not in a mild and moderate way, but with their
whole hearts. This is a legitimate result of habit
and education. Our nation will like the opera, too,
by and by, no doubt. One in fifty of those who

attend our operas likes it already, perhaps, but I think a good many of the other forty-nine go in order to learn to like it, and the rest in order to be able to talk knowingly about it. The latter usually hum the airs while they are being sung, so that their neighbors may perceive that they have been to operas before. The funerals of these do not occur often enough.

A gentle, old-maidish person and a sweet young girl of seventeen sat right in front of us that night at the Mannheim opera. These people talked, between the acts, and I understood them, though I understood nothing that was uttered on the distant stage. At first they were guarded in their talk, but after they had heard my agent and me conversing in English they dropped their reserve and I picked up many of their little confidences; no, I mean many of *her* little confidences—meaning the elder party —for the young girl only listened, and gave assenting nods, but never said a word. How pretty she was, and how sweet she was! I wished she would speak. But evidently she was absorbed in her own thoughts, her own young-girl dreams, and found a dearer pleasure in silence. But she was not dreaming sleepy dreams—no, she was awake, alive, alert, she could not sit still a moment. She was an enchanting study. Her gown was of a soft white silky stuff that clung to her round young figure like a fish's skin, and it was rippled over with the gracefulest little fringy films of lace; she had deep, tender eyes, with long, curved lashes; and she had peachy cheeks, and a dimpled chin, and such a dear little dewy rosebud of a mouth; and she was so dovelike, so pure, and so gracious, so sweet and bewitching. For long hours I did mightily wish she would speak. And at last she did; the red lips parted, and out leaped her thought—and with such a guileless and pretty enthusiasm, too: "Auntie, I just *know* I've got five hundred fleas on me!"

That was probably over the average. Yes, it must have been very much over the average. The average at that time in the Grand Duchy of Baden was forty-five to a young person (when alone), according to the official estimate of the home secretary for that year; the average for older people was shifty and indeterminable, for whenever a wholesome young girl came into the presence of her elders she immediately lowered their average and raised her own. She became a sort of contribution-box. This dear young thing in the theater had been sitting there unconsciously taking up a collection. Many a skinny old being in our neighborhood was the happier and the restfuler for her coming.

In that large audience, that night, there were eight very conspicuous people. These were ladies who had their hats or bonnets on. What a blessed thing it would be if a lady could make herself conspicuous in our theaters by wearing her hat. It is not usual in Europe to allow ladies and gentlemen to take bonnets, hats, overcoats, canes, or umbrellas into the auditorium, but in Mannheim this rule was not enforced because the audiences were largely made up of people from a distance, and among these were always a few timid ladies who were afraid that if

A TRAMP ABROAD

they had to go into an anteroom to get their things when the play was over, they would miss their train. But the great mass of those who came from a distance always ran the risk and took the chances, preferring the loss of the train to a breach of good manners and the discomfort of being unpleasantly conspicuous during a stretch of three or four hours.

CHAPTER X

THREE or four hours. That is a long time to sit in one place, whether one be conspicuous or not, yet some of Wagner's operas bang along for six whole hours on a stretch! But the people sit there and enjoy it all, and wish it would last longer. A German lady in Munich told me that a person could not like Wagner's music at first, but must go through the deliberate process of learning to like it—then he would have his sure reward; for when he had learned to like it he would hunger for it and never be able to get enough of it. She said that six hours of Wagner was by no means too much. She said that this composer had made a complete revolution in music and was burying the old masters one by one. And she said that Wagner's operas differed from all others in one notable respect, and that was that they were not merely spotted with music here and there, but were *all* music, from the first strain to the last. This surprised me. I said I had attended one of his insurrections, and found hardly *any* music in it except the Wedding Chorus. She said "Lohengrin" was noisier than Wagner's other operas, but that if I would keep on going to see it I would find by and by that it was all music, and therefore would then enjoy it. I *could* have said,

"But would you advise a person to deliberately practise having the toothache in the pit of his stomach for a couple of years in order that he might then come to enjoy it?" But I reserved that remark.

This lady was full of the praises of the head-tenor who had performed in a Wagner opera the night before, and went on to enlarge upon his old and prodigious fame, and how many honors had been lavished upon him by the princely houses of Germany. Here was another surprise. I had attended that very opera, in the person of my agent, and had made close and accurate observations. So I said:

"Why, madam, *my* experience warrants me in stating that that tenor's voice is not a voice at all, but only a shriek—the shriek of a hyena."

"That is very true," she said; "he cannot sing now; it is already many years that he has lost his voice, but in other times he sang, yes, divinely! So whenever he comes now, you shall see, yes, that the theater will not hold the people. *Jawohl bei Gott!* his voice is *wunderschön* in that past time."

I said she was discovering to me a kindly trait in the Germans which was worth emulating. I said that over the water we were not quite so generous; that with us, when a singer had lost his voice and a jumper had lost his legs, these parties ceased to draw. I said I had been to the opera in Hanover, once, and in Mannheim once, and in Munich (through my authorized agent) once, and this large experience had nearly persuaded me that the Germans *preferred* singers who couldn't sing. This was not such a very extravagant speech, either, for that burly Mannheim tenor's praises had been the talk of all Heidelberg for a week before his performance took place—yet his voice was like the distressing noise which a nail makes when you screech it across a window-pane. I said so to Heidelberg friends the next day, and they said, in the calmest and simplest way, that that was very true, but that in earlier times his voice *had* been wonderfully fine. And the tenor in Hanover was just another example of this sort. The English-speaking German gentleman who went with me to the opera there was brimming with enthusiasm over that tenor. He said:

"*Ach Gott!* a great man! You shall see him. He is so celebrate in all Germany—and he has a pension, yes, from the government. He not obliged to sing now, only twice every year; but if he not sing twice each year they take him his pension away."

Very well, we went. When the renowned old tenor appeared, I got a nudge and an excited whisper:

"Now you see him!"

But the "celebrate" was an astonishing disappointment to me. If he had been behind a screen I should have supposed they were performing a surgical operation on him. I looked at my friend— to my great surprise he seemed intoxicated with pleasure, his eyes were dancing with eager delight. When the curtain at last fell, he burst into the stormiest applause, and kept it up—as did the whole house—until the afflictive tenor had come three times before the curtain to make his bow.

A TRAMP ABROAD

While the glowing enthusiast was swabbing the perspiration from his face, I said:

"I don't mean the least harm, but really, now, do you think he can sing?"

"Him? *No! Gott im Himmel, aber,* how he has been able to sing twenty-five years ago?" [Then pensively.] "*Ach*, no, *now* he not sing any more, he only cry. When he think he sing, now, he not sing at all, no, he only make like a cat which is unwell."

Where and how did we get the idea that the Germans are a stolid, phlegmatic race? In truth, they are widely removed from that. They are warm-hearted, emotional, impulsive, enthusiastic, their tears come at the mildest touch, and it is not hard to move them to laughter. They are the very children of impulse. We are cold and self-contained, compared to the Germans. They hug and kiss and cry and shout and dance and sing; and where we use one loving, petting expression they pour out a score. Their language is full of endearing diminutives; nothing that they love escapes the application of a petting diminutive—neither the house, nor the dog, nor the horse, nor the grandmother, nor any other creature, animate or inanimate.

In the theaters at Hanover, Hamburg, and Mannheim, they had a wise custom. The moment the curtain went up, the lights in the body of the house went down. The audience sat in the cool gloom of a deep twilight, which greatly enhanced the glowing splendors of the stage. It saved gas, too, and people were not sweated to death.

When I saw "King Lear" played, nobody was allowed to see a scene shifted; if there was nothing to be done but slide a forest out of the way and expose a temple beyond, one did not see that forest split itself in the middle and go shrieking away, with the accompanying disenchanting spectacle of the hands and heels of the impelling impulse—no, the curtain was always dropped for an instant—one heard not the least movement behind it—but when it went up, the next instant, the forest was gone. Even when the stage was being entirely reset, one heard no noise. During the whole time that "King Lear" was playing the curtain was never down two minutes at any one time. The orchestra played until the curtain was ready to go up for the first time, then they departed for the evening. Where the stage-waits never reach two minutes there is no occasion for music. I had never seen this two-minute business between acts but once before, and that was when the "Shaughraun" was played at Wallack's.

I was at a concert in Munich one night, the people were streaming in, the clock-hand pointed to seven, the music struck up, and instantly all movement in the body of the house ceased—nobody was standing, or walking up the aisles, or fumbling with a seat, the stream of incomers had suddenly dried up at its source. I listened undisturbed to a piece of music that was fifteen minutes long—always expecting some tardy ticket-holders to come crowding past my knees, and being continuously and pleasantly disappointed—but when the last note was struck, here came the stream again. You see, they had made those late comers wait in the comfortable waiting-parlor from the time the music had begun until it was ended.

It was the first time I had ever seen this sort of criminals denied the privilege of destroying the comfort of a house full of their betters. Some of these were pretty fine birds, but no matter, they had to tarry outside in the long parlor under the inspection of a double rank of liveried footmen and waiting-maids who supported the two walls with their backs and held the wraps and traps of their masters and mistresses on their arms.

We had no footmen to hold our things, and it was not permissible to take them into the concert-room; but there were some men and women to take charge of them for us. They gave us checks for them and charged a fixed price, payable in advance— five cents.

In Germany they always hear one thing at an opera which has never yet been heard in America, perhaps—I mean the closing strain of a fine solo or duet. We always smash into it with an earth-quake of applause. The result is that we rob ourselves of the sweetest part of the treat; we get the whisky, but we don't get the sugar in the bottom of the glass.

Our way of scattering applause along through an act seems to me to be better than the Mannheim way of saving it all up till the act is ended. I do not see how an actor can forget himself and portray hot passion before a cold still audience. I should think he would feel foolish. It is a pain to me to

6

this day, to remember how that old German Lear raged and wept and howled around the stage, with never a response from that hushed house, never a single outburst till the act was ended. To me there was something unspeakably uncomfortable in the solemn dead silences that always followed this old person's tremendous outpourings of his feelings. I could not help putting myself in his place—I thought I knew how sick and flat he felt during those silences, because I remembered a case which came under my observation once, and which—but I will tell the incident:

One evening on board a Mississippi steamboat, a boy of ten years lay asleep in a berth—a long, slim-legged boy, he was, encased in quite a short shirt; it was the first time he had ever made a trip on a steamboat, and so he was troubled, and scared, and had gone to bed with his head filled with impending snaggings, and explosions, and conflagra-tions, and sudden death. About ten o'clock some twenty ladies were sitting around about the ladies' saloon, quietly reading, sewing, embroidering, and so on, and among them sat a sweet, benignant old dame with round spectacles on her nose and her busy knitting-needles in her hands. Now all of a sudden, into the midst of this peaceful scene burst that slim-shanked boy in the brief shirt, wild-eyed, erect-haired, and shouting, "Fire, fire! *jump and run, the boat's afire and there ain't a minute to lose!*" All those ladies looked sweetly up and smiled, nobody stirred, the old lady pulled her spectacles down, looked over them, and said, gently:

"But you mustn't catch cold, child. Run and put on your breastpin, and then come and tell us all about it."

It was a cruel chill to give to a poor little devil's gushing vehemence. He was expecting to be a sort of hero—the creator of a wild panic—and here everybody sat and smiled a mocking smile, and an old woman made fun of his bugbear. I turned and crept humbly away—for I was that boy—and never even cared to discover whether I had dreamed the fire or actually seen it.

I am told that in a German concert or opera, they hardly ever encore a song; that though they may be dying to hear it again, their good breeding usually preserves them against requiring the repetition.

Kings may encore; that is quite another matter; it delights everybody to see that the King is pleased; and as to the actor encored, his pride and gratification are simply boundless. Still, there are circumstances in which even a royal encore—

But it is better to illustrate. The King of Bavaria is a poet, and has a poet's eccentricities—with the advantage over all other poets of being able to gratify them, no matter what form they may take. He is fond of the opera, but not fond of sitting in the presence of an audience; therefore, it has sometimes occurred, in Munich, that when an opera has been concluded and the players were getting off their paint and finery, a command has come to them to get their paint and finery on again. Presently the King would arrive, solitary and alone, and the players would begin at the beginning and do the entire opera over again with only that one individual in the vast solemn theater for audience. Once he took an odd freak into his head. High up and out of sight, over the prodigious stage of the court theater is a maze of interlacing water-pipes, so pierced that in case of fire, innumerable little thread-like streams of water can be caused to descend; and in case of need, this discharge can be augmented to a pouring flood. American managers might make a note of that. The King was sole audience. The opera proceeded, it was a piece with a storm in it; the mimic thunder began to mutter, the mimic wind began to wail and sough, and the mimic rain to patter. The King's interest rose higher and higher; it developed into enthusiasm. He cried out:

"It is good, very good, indeed! But I will have real rain! Turn on the water!"

The manager pleaded for a reversal of the command; said it would ruin the costly scenery and the splendid costumes, but the King cried:

"No matter, no matter, I will have real rain! Turn on the water!"

So the real rain was turned on and began to descend in gossamer lances to the mimic flower-beds and gravel walks of the stage. The richly dressed actresses and actors tripped about singing bravely and pretending not to mind it. The King was delighted—his enthusiasm grew higher. He cried out:

"Bravo, bravo! More thunder! more lightning! turn on more rain!"

The thunder boomed, the lightning glared, the

storm-winds raged, the deluge poured down. The mimic royalty on the stage, with their soaked satins clinging to their bodies, slopped around ankle-deep in water, warbling their sweetest and best, the fiddlers under the eaves of the stage sawed away for dear life, with the cold overflow spouting down the backs of their necks, and the dry and happy King sat in his lofty box and wore his gloves to ribbons applauding.

"More yet!" cried the King; "more yet—let loose all the thunder, turn on all the water! I will hang the man that raises an umbrella!"

When this most tremendous and effective storm that had ever been produced in any theater was at last over, the King's approbation was measureless. He cried:

"Magnificent, magnificent! *Encore!* Do it again!"

But the manager succeeded in persuading him to recall the encore, and said the company would feel sufficiently rewarded and complimented in the mere fact that the encore was desired by his Majesty, without fatiguing him with a repetition to gratify their own vanity.

During the remainder of the act the lucky performers were those whose parts required changes of dress; the others were a soaked, bedraggled, and uncomfortable lot, but in the last degree picturesque. The stage scenery was ruined, trap-doors were so swollen that they wouldn't work for a week afterward, the fine costumes were spoiled, and no end of minor damages were done by that remarkable storm.

It was a royal idea—that storm—and royally

carried out. But observe the moderation of the King; he did not insist upon his encore. If he had been a gladsome, unreflecting American opera-audience, he probably would have had his storm repeated and repeated until he drowned all those people.

CHAPTER XI

THE summer days passed pleasantly in Heidelberg. We had a skilled trainer, and under his
instructions we were getting our legs in the right
condition for the contemplated pedestrian tours; we
were well satisfied with the progress which we had
made in the German language,[1] and more than
satisfied with what we had accomplished in art.
We had had the best instructors in drawing and
painting in Germany—Hämmerling, Vogel, Müller,
Dietz, and Schumann. Hämmerling taught us landscape - painting, Vogel taught us figure - drawing,
Müller taught us to do still-life, and Dietz and
Schumann gave us a finishing course in two specialties — battle - pieces and shipwrecks. Whatever I
am in Art I owe to these men. I have something
of the manner of each and all of them; but they all
said that I had also a manner of my own, and that
it was conspicuous. They said there was a marked
individuality about my style—insomuch that if I
ever painted the commonest type of a dog, I should
be sure to throw a something into the aspect of that
dog which would keep him from being mistaken for
the creation of any other artist. Secretly I wanted
to believe all these kind sayings, but I could not; I

[1] See Appendix D for information concerning this fearful tongue.

was afraid that my masters' partiality for me, and pride in me, biased their judgment. So I resolved to make a test. Privately, and unknown to any one, I painted my great picture, "Heidelberg Castle Illuminated"—my first really important work in oils—and had it hung up in the midst of a wilderness of oil-pictures in the Art Exhibition, with no name attached to it. To my great gratification it was instantly recognized as mine. All the town flocked to see it, and people even came from neighboring localities to visit it. It made more stir than any other work in the Exhibition. But the most gratifying thing of all was, that chance strangers, passing through, who had not heard of my picture, were not only drawn to it, as by a lodestone, the moment they entered the gallery, but always took it for a "Turner."

Mr. Harris was graduated in Art about the same time with myself, and we took a studio together. We waited awhile for some orders; then as time began to drag a little, we concluded to make a pedestrian tour. After much consideration, we determined on a trip up the shores of the beautiful Neckar to Heilbronn. Apparently nobody had ever done that. There were ruined castles on the overhanging cliffs and crags all the way; these were said to have their legends, like those on the Rhine, and what was better still, they had never been in print. There was nothing in the books about that lovely region; it had been neglected by the tourist, it was virgin soil for the literary pioneer.

Meantime the knapsacks, the rough walking-suits

and the stout walking-shoes which we had ordered, were finished and brought to us. A Mr. X and a young Mr. Z had agreed to go with us. We went around one evening and bade good-by to our friends, and afterward had a little farewell banquet at the hotel. We got to bed early, for we wanted to make an early start, so as to take advantage of the cool of the morning.

We were out of bed at break of day, feeling fresh and vigorous, and took a hearty breakfast, then plunged down through the leafy arcades of the Castle grounds, toward the town. What a glorious summer morning it was, and how the flowers did pour out their fragrance, and how the birds did sing! It was just the time for a tramp through the woods and mountains.

We were all dressed alike: broad slouch hats, to keep the sun off; gray knapsacks; blue army shirts; blue overalls; leathern gaiters buttoned tight from knee down to ankle; high-quarter coarse shoes snugly laced. Each man had an opera-glass, a canteen, and a guide-book case slung over his shoulder, and carried an alpenstock in one hand and a sun-umbrella in the other. Around our hats were wound many folds of soft white muslin, with the ends hanging and flapping down our backs—an idea brought from the Orient and used by tourists all over Europe. Harris carried the little watch-like machine called a "pedometer," whose office is to keep count of a man's steps and tell how far he has walked. Everybody stopped to admire our costumes and give us a hearty "Pleasant march to you!"

When we got down-town I found that we could go by rail to within five miles of Heilbronn. The train was just starting, so we jumped aboard and went tearing away in splendid spirits. It was agreed all around that we had done wisely, because it would be just as enjoyable to walk *down* the Neckar as up it, and it could not be needful to walk both ways. There were some nice German people in our compartment. I got to talking some pretty private matters presently, and Harris became nervous; so he nudged me and said:

"Speak in German—these Germans may understand English."

I did so, and it was well I did; for it turned out that there was not a German in that party who did not understand English perfectly. It is curious how wide-spread our language is in Germany. After a while some of those folks got out and a German gentleman and his two young daughters got in. I spoke in German to one of the latter several times, but without result. Finally she said:

"*Ich verstehe nur Deutch und Englishe,*"—or words to that effect. That is, "I don't understand any language but German and English."

And sure enough, not only she but her father and sister spoke English. So after that we had all the talk we wanted; and we wanted a good deal, for they were very agreeable people. They were greatly interested in our costumes; especially the alpenstocks, for they had not seen any before. They said that the Neckar road was perfectly level, so we must be going to Switzerland or some other rugged country; and asked us if we did not find the walking pretty fatiguing in such warm weather. But we said no.

We reached Wimpfen—I think it was Wimpfen —in about three hours, and got out, not the least tired; found a good hotel and ordered beer and dinner—then took a stroll through the venerable old village. It was very picturesque and tumble-down, and dirty and interesting. It had queer houses five hundred years old in it, and a military tower, 115 feet high, which had stood there more than ten centuries. I made a little sketch of it. I kept a copy, but gave the original to the Burgomaster. I think the original was better than the copy, be-

THE TOWER

cause it had more windows in it and the grass stood up better and had a brisker look. There was none around the tower, though; I composed the grass myself, from studies I made in a field by Heidelberg in Hämmerling's time. The man on top, looking at the view, is apparently too large, but I found he could not be made smaller, conveniently. I wanted him there, and I wanted him visible, so I thought out a way to manage it; I composed the picture from two points of view; the spectator is to observe the man from about where that flag is, and he must observe the tower itself from the ground. This harmonizes the seeming discrepancy.

Near an old cathedral, under a shed, were three crosses of stone—moldy and damaged things, bearing life-size stone figures. The two thieves were dressed in the fanciful court costumes of the middle of the sixteenth century, while the Saviour was nude, with the exception of a cloth around the loins.

We had dinner under the green trees in a garden belonging to the hotel and overlooking the Neckar; then, after a smoke, we went to bed. We had a refreshing nap, then got up about three in the afternoon and put on our panoply. As we tramped gaily out at the gate of the town, we overtook a peasant's cart, partly laden with odds and ends of cabbages and similar vegetable rubbish, and drawn by a small cow and a smaller donkey yoked together. It was a pretty slow concern, but it got us into Heilbronn before dark—five miles, or possibly it was seven.

We stopped at the very same inn which the famous old robber-knight and rough fighter, Götz von Berlichingen, abode in after he got out of captivity in the Square Tower of Heilbronn between three hundred and fifty and four hundred years ago. Harris and I occupied the same room which he had occupied and the same paper had not all peeled off the walls yet. The furniture was quaint old carved stuff, full four hundred years old, and some of the smells were over a thousand. There was a hook in the wall, which the landlord said the terrific old Götz used to hang his iron hand on when he took it off to go to bed. This room was very large—it might be called immense—and it was on the first floor; which means it was in the second story, for in Europe the houses are so high that they do not count the first story, else they would get tired climbing before they got to the top. The wall-paper was a fiery red, with huge gold figures in it, well smirched by time, and it covered all the doors. These doors fitted so snugly and continued the figures of the paper so unbrokenly, that when they were closed one had to go feeling and searching along the wall to find them. There was a stove in the corner—one of those tall, square, stately white porcelain things that looks like a monument and keeps you thinking of death when you ought to be enjoying your travels. The windows looked out on a little alley, and over that into a stable and some poultry and pig yards in the rear of some tenement-houses. There were the customary two beds in the room, one in one end of it, the other in the other, about an old-fashioned brass-mounted, single-barreled pistol-shot apart. They were fully as narrow as the usual German bed, too, and had the German bed's ineradicable habit of spilling the blankets on the floor every time you forgot yourself and went to sleep.

A round table as large as King Arthur's stood in the center of the room; while the waiters were getting ready to serve our dinner on it we all went out to see the renowned clock on the front of the municipal buildings.

CHAPTER XII

THE *Rathhaus*, or municipal building, is of the quaintest and most picturesque Middle - Age architecture. It has a massive portico and steps, before it, heavily balustraded, and adorned with life-size rusty iron knights in complete armor. The clock-face on the front of the building is very large and of curious pattern. Ordinarily, a gilded angel strikes the hour on a big bell with a hammer; as the striking ceases, a life-size figure of Time raises its hour-glass and turns it; two golden rams advance and butt each other; a gilded cock lifts its wings; but the main features are two great angels, who stand on each side of the dial with long horns at their lips; it was said that they blew melodious blasts on these horns every hour—but they did not do it for us. We were told, later, that they blew only at night, when the town was still.

Within the *Rathhaus* were a number of huge wild boars' heads, preserved, and mounted on brackets along the wall; they bore inscriptions telling who killed them and how many hundred years ago it was done. One room in the building was devoted to the preservation of ancient archives. There they showed us no end of aged documents; some were signed by Popes, some by Tilly and other great generals, and one was a letter written and subscribed by Götz von Berlichingen in Heilbronn in 1519 just after his release from the Square Tower.

This fine old robber-knight was a devoutly and sincerely religious man, hospitable, charitable to the poor, fearless in fight, active, enterprising, and possessed of a large and generous nature. He had in him a quality which was rare in that rough time—the quality of being able to overlook moderate injuries, and of being able to forgive and forget mortal ones as soon as he had soundly trounced the authors of them. He was prompt to take up any poor devil's quarrel and risk his neck to right him. The common folk held him dear, and his memory is still green in ballad and tradition. He used to go on the highway and rob rich wayfarers; and other times he would swoop down from his high castle on the hills of the Neckar and capture passing cargoes of merchandise. In his memoirs he piously thanks the Giver of all Good for remembering him in his needs and delivering sundry such cargoes into his hands at times when only special providences could have relieved him. He was a doughty warrior and found a deep joy in battle. In an assault upon a stronghold in Bavaria when he was only twenty-three years old, his right hand was shot away, but he was so interested in the fight that he did not observe it for a while. He said that the iron hand which was made for him afterward, and which he wore for more than half a century, was nearly as clever a member as the fleshy one had been. I was glad to get a facsimile of the letter written by this fine old German Robin Hood, though I was not able to read it. He was a better artist with his sword than with his pen.

We went down by the river and saw the Square Tower. It was a very venerable structure, very strong, and very ornamental. There was no opening near the ground. They had to use a ladder to get into it, no doubt.

We visited the principal church, also—a curious old structure, with a towerlike spire adorned with all sorts of grotesque images. The inner walls of the church were placarded with large mural tablets of copper, bearing engraved inscriptions celebrating the merits of old Heilbronn worthies of two or three centuries ago, and also bearing rudely painted effigies of themselves and their families tricked out in the queer costumes of those days. The head of the family sat in the foreground, and beyond him extended a sharply receding and diminishing row of sons; facing him sat his wife, and beyond her extended a long row of diminishing daughters. The family was usually large, but the perspective bad.

Then we hired the hack and the horse which Götz von Berlichingen used to use, and drove several miles into the country to visit the place called *Weibertreu*—Wife's Fidelity I suppose it means. It was a feudal castle of the Middle Ages. When we reached its neighborhood we found it was beautifully situated, but on top of a mound, or hill, round and tolerably steep, and about two hundred feet high. Therefore, as the sun was blazing hot, we did not climb up there, but took the place on trust, and observed it from a distance while the horse leaned up against a fence and rested. The place has no interest except that which is lent it by its legend, which is a very pretty one—to this effect:

THE LEGEND

In the Middle Ages, a couple of young dukes, brothers, took opposite sides in one of the wars, the one fighting for the Emperor, the other against him. One of them owned the castle and village on top of the mound which I have been speaking of, and in his absence his brother came with his knights and soldiers and began a siege. It was a long and tedious business, for the people made a stubborn and faithful defense. But at last their supplies ran out and starvation began its work; more fell by hunger than by the missiles of the enemy. They by and by surrendered, and begged for charitable terms. But the beleaguering prince was so incensed against them for their long resistance that he said he would spare none but the women and children—all the men should be put to the sword without exception, and all their goods destroyed. Then the women came and fell on their knees and begged for the lives of their husbands.

"No," said the prince, "not a man of them shall escape alive; you yourselves shall go with your children into houseless and friendless banishment; but that you may not starve I grant you this one grace, that each woman may bear with her from this place as much of her most valuable property as she is able to carry."

Very well, presently the gates swung open and out filed those women carrying their *husbands* on their shoulders. The besiegers, furious at the trick, rushed forward to slaughter the men, but the Duke stepped between and said:

"No, put up your swords—a prince's word is inviolable."

When we got back to the hotel, King Arthur's Round Table was ready for us in its white drapery, and the head waiter and his first assistant, in swallow-tails and white cravats, brought in the soup and the hot plates at once.

Mr. X had ordered the dinner, and when the wine came on, he picked up a bottle, glanced at the label, and then turned to the grave, the melancholy, the sepulchral head waiter and said it was not the sort of wine he had asked for. The head waiter picked up the bottle, cast his undertaker-eye on it and said:

"It is true; I beg pardon." Then he turned on his subordinate and calmly said, "Bring another label."

At the same time he slid the present label off with his hand and laid it aside; it had been newly put on, its paste was still wet. When the new label came, he put it on; our French wine being now turned into German wine, according to desire, the head waiter went blandly about his other duties, as if the working of this sort of miracle was a common and easy thing to him.

Mr. X said he had not known, before, that there were people honest enough to do this miracle in public, but he was aware that thousands upon thousands of labels were imported into America from Europe every year, to enable dealers to furnish to their customers in a quiet and inexpensive way all the different kinds of foreign wines they might require.

We took a turn around the town, after dinner, and found it fully as interesting in the moonlight as it had been in the daytime. The streets were narrow and roughly paved, and there was not a sidewalk or a street-lamp anywhere. The dwellings were centuries old, and vast enough for hotels. They widened all the way up; the stories projected further and further forward and aside as they ascended, and the long rows of lighted windows, filled with little bits of panes, curtained with figured white muslin and adorned outside with boxes of flowers, made a pretty effect. The moon was bright, and the light and shadow very strong; and nothing could be more picturesque than those curving streets, with their rows of huge high gables leaning far over toward each other in a friendly gossiping way, and the crowds below drifting through the alternating blots of gloom and mellow bars of moonlight. Nearly everybody was abroad, chatting, singing, romping, or massed in lazy comfortable attitudes in the doorways.

In one place there was a public building which was fenced about with a thick, rusty chain, which sagged from post to post in a succession of low swings. The pavement, here, was made of heavy blocks of stone. In the glare of the moon a party of barefooted children were swinging on those chains and having a noisy good time. They were not the first ones who had done that; even their great-great-grandfathers had not been the first to do it when they were children. The strokes of the bare feet had worn grooves inches deep in the stone flags; it had taken many generations of swinging children to accomplish that. Everywhere in the town were the mold and decay that go with antiquity, and evidence it; but I do not know that anything else gave us so vivid a sense of the old age of Heilbronn as those footworn grooves in the paving-stones.

CHAPTER XIII

WHEN we got back to the hotel I wound and set the pedometer and put it in my pocket, for I was to carry it next day and keep record of the miles we made. The work which we had given the instrument to do during the day which had just closed had not fatigued it perceptibly.

We were in bed by ten, for we wanted to be up and away on our tramp homeward with the dawn. I hung fire, but Harris went to sleep at once. I hate a man who goes to sleep at once; there is a sort of indefinable something about it which is not exactly an insult, and yet is an insolence; and one which is hard to bear, too. I lay there fretting over this injury, and trying to go to sleep; but the harder I tried, the wider awake I grew. I got to feeling very lonely in the dark, with no company but an undigested dinner. My mind got a start by and by, and began to consider the beginning of every subject which has ever been thought of; but it never went further than the beginning; it was touch and go; it fled from topic to topic with a frantic speed. At the end of an hour my head was in a perfect whirl and I was dead tired, fagged out.

The fatigue was so great that it presently began to make some head against the nervous excitement;

while imagining myself wide awake, I would really doze into momentary unconsciousness, and come suddenly out of it with a physical jerk which nearly wrenched my joints apart—the delusion of the instant being that I was tumbling backward over a precipice. After I had fallen over eight or nine precipices and thus found out that one half of my brain had been asleep eight or nine times without the wide-awake, hard-working other half suspecting it, the periodical unconsciousnesses began to extend their spell gradually over more of my brain-territory, and at last I sank into a drowse which grew deeper and deeper and was doubtless just on the very point of becoming a solid, blessed dreamless stupor, when—what was that?

My dulled faculties dragged themselves partly back to life and took a receptive attitude. Now out of an immense, a limitless distance, came a something which grew and grew, and approached, and presently was recognizable as a sound—it had rather seemed to be a feeling, before. This sound was a mile away, now—perhaps it was the murmur of a storm; and now it was nearer—not a quarter of a mile away; was it the muffled rasping and grinding of distant machinery? No, it came still nearer; was it the measured tramp of a marching troop? But it came nearer still, and still nearer—and at last it was right in the room: it was merely a mouse gnawing the woodwork. So I had held my breath all that time for such a trifle.

Well, what was done could not be helped; I would go to sleep at once and make up the lost time. That was a thoughtless thought. Without intending it—hardly knowing it—I fell to listening intently to that sound, and even unconsciously counting the strokes of the mouse's nutmeg-grater. Presently I was deriving exquisite suffering from this employment, yet maybe I could have endured it if the mouse had attended steadily to his work; but he did not do that; he stopped every now and then, and I suffered more while waiting and listening for him to begin again than I did while he was gnawing. Along at first I was mentally offering a reward of five—six—seven—ten—dollars for that mouse; but toward the last I was offering rewards which were entirely beyond my means. I close-reefed my ears—that is to say, I bent the flaps of them down and furled them into five or six folds, and pressed them against the hearing-orifice—but it did no good: the faculty was so sharpened by nervous excitement that it was become a microphone and could hear through the overlays without trouble.

My anger grew to a frenzy. I finally did what all persons before me have done, clear back to Adam, —resolved to throw something. I reached down and got my walking-shoes, then sat up in bed and listened, in order to exactly locate the noise. But I couldn't do it; it was as unlocatable as a cricket's noise; and where one thinks that that is, is always the very place where it isn't. So I presently hurled a shoe at random, and with a vicious vigor. It struck the wall over Harris's head and fell down on him; I had not imagined I could throw so far. It woke Harris, and I was glad of it until I found he was not angry;

then I was sorry. He soon went to sleep again, which pleased me; but straightway the mouse began again, which roused my temper once more. I did not want to wake Harris a second time, but the gnawing continued until I was compelled to throw the other shoe. This time I broke a mirror—there were two in the room—I got the largest one, of course. Harris woke again, but did not complain, and I was sorrier than ever. I resolved that I would suffer all possible torture before I would disturb him a third time.

The mouse eventually retired, and by and by I was sinking to sleep, when a clock began to strike; I counted till it was done, and was about to drowse again when another clock began; I counted; then the two great *Rathhaus* clock angels began to send forth soft, rich, melodious blasts from their long trumpets. I had never heard anything that was so lovely, or weird, or mysterious—but when they got to blowing the quarter-hours, they seemed to me to be overdoing the thing. Every time I dropped off for a moment, a new noise woke me. Each time I woke I missed my coverlet, and had to reach down to the floor and get it again.

At last all sleepiness forsook me. I recognized the fact that I was hopelessly and permanently wide awake. Wide awake, and feverish and thirsty. When I had lain tossing there as long as I could endure it, it occurred to me that it would be a good idea to dress and go out in the great square and take a refreshing wash in the fountain, and smoke and reflect there until the remnant of the night was gone.

I believed I could dress in the dark without waking Harris. I had banished my shoes after the mouse, but my slippers would do for a summer night. So I rose softly, and gradually got on everything— down to one sock. I couldn't seem to get on the track of that sock, any way I could fix it. But I had to have it; so I went down on my hands and knees, with one slipper on and the other in my hand, and began to paw gently around and rake the floor, but with no success. I enlarged my circle, and went on pawing and raking. With every pressure of my knee, how the floor creaked! and every time I chanced to rake against any article, it seemed to give out thirty-five or thirty-six times more noise than it would have done in the daytime. In those cases I always stopped and held my breath till I was sure Harris had not awakened—then I crept along again. I moved on and on, but I could not find the sock; I could not seem to find anything but furniture. I could not remember that there was much furniture in the room when I went to bed, but the place was alive with it now—especially chairs—chairs everywhere—had a couple of families moved in, in the mean time? And I never could seem to *glance* on one of those chairs, but always struck it full and square with my head. My temper rose, by steady and sure degrees, and as I pawed on and on, I fell to making vicious comments under my breath.

Finally, with a venomous access of irritation, I said I would leave without the sock; so I rose up and made straight for the door—as I supposed—and suddenly confronted my dim spectral image in the unbroken mirror. It startled the breath out of me, for an instant; it also showed me that I was lost, and had no sort of idea where I was. When I realized this, I was so angry that I had to sit down on the floor and take hold of something to keep from lifting the roof off with an explosion of opinion. If there had been only one mirror, it might possibly have helped to locate me; but there were two, and two were as bad as a thousand; besides, these were on opposite sides of the room. I could see the dim blur of the windows, but in my turned-around condition they were exactly where they ought not to be, and so they only confused me instead of helping me.

I started to get up, and knocked down an umbrella; it made a noise like a pistol-shot when it struck that hard, slick, carpetless floor; I grated my teeth and held my breath—Harris did not stir. I set the umbrella slowly and carefully on end against the wall, but as soon as I took my hand away, its heel slipped from under it, and down it came again with another bang. I shrunk together and listened a moment in silent fury—no harm done, everything quiet. With the most painstaking care and nicety I stood the umbrella up once more, took my hand away, and down it came again.

I have been strictly reared, but if it had not been so dark and solemn and awful there in that lonely, vast room, I do believe I should have said something then which could not be put into a Sunday-school book without injuring the sale of it. If my reasoning powers had not been already sapped dry by my harassments, I would have known better than to try to set an umbrella on end on one of those glassy German floors in the dark; it can't be done in the daytime without four failures to one success. I had one comfort, though—Harris was yet still and silent—he had not stirred.

The umbrella could not locate me—there were four standing around the room, and all alike. I thought I would feel along the wall and find the door in that way. I rose up and began this operation, but raked down a picture. It was not a large one, but it made noise enough for a panorama. Harris gave out no sound, but I felt that if I experimented any further with the pictures I should be sure to wake him. Better give up trying to get out. Yes, I would find King Arthur's Round Table once more —I had already found it several times—and use it for a base of departure on an exploring tour for my bed; if I could find my bed I could then find my water pitcher; I would quench my raging thirst and turn in. So I started on my hands and knees, because I could go faster that way, and with more confidence, too, and not knock down things. By and by I found the table—with my head—rubbed the bruise a little, then rose up and started, with hands abroad and fingers spread, to balance myself. I found a chair; then the wall; then another chair; then a sofa; then an alpenstock, then another sofa; this confounded me, for I had thought there was only one sofa. I hunted up the table again and took a fresh start; found some more chairs.

It occurred to me, now, as it ought to have done

before, that as the table was round, it was therefore of no value as a base to aim from; so I moved off once more, and at random among the wilderness of chairs and sofas — wandered off into unfamiliar regions, and presently knocked a candlestick off a mantelpiece; grabbed at the candlestick and knocked off a lamp, grabbed at the lamp and knocked off a water pitcher with a rattling crash, and thought to myself, "I've found you at last—I judged I was close upon you." Harris shouted "murder," and "thieves," and finished with "I'm absolutely drowned."

The crash had roused the house. Mr. X pranced in, in his long night-garment, with a candle, young Z after him with another candle; a procession swept in at another door, with candles and lanterns—landlord and two German guests in their nightgowns, and a chambermaid in hers.

I looked around; I was at Harris's bed, a Sabbath-day's journey from my own. There was only one sofa; it was against the wall; there was only one chair where a body could get at it—I had been revolving around it like a planet, and colliding with it like a comet half the night.

I explained how I had been employing myself, and why. Then the landlord's party left, and the rest of us set about our preparations for breakfast, for the dawn was ready to break. I glanced furtively at my pedometer, and found I had made 47 miles. But I did not care, for I had come out for a pedestrian tour anyway.

CHAPTER XIV

WHEN the landlord learned that I and my agents were artists, our party rose perceptibly in his esteem; we rose still higher when he learned that we were making a pedestrian tour of Europe.

He told us all about the Heidelberg road, and which were the best places to avoid and which the best ones to tarry at; he charged me less than cost for the things I broke in the night; he put up a fine luncheon for us and added to it a quantity of great light-green plums, the pleasantest fruit in Germany; he was so anxious to do us honor that he would not allow us to walk out of Heilbronn, but called up Götz von Berlichingen's horse and cab and made us ride.

I made a sketch of the turnout. It is not a Work, it is only what artists call a "study"—a thing to make a finished picture from. This sketch has several blemishes in it; for instance, the wagon is not traveling as fast as the horse is. This is wrong. Again, the person trying to get out of the way is too small; he is out of perspective, as we say. The two upper lines are not the horse's back, they are the reins; there seems to be a wheel missing—this would be corrected in a finished Work, of

Leaving Heilbronn

course. That thing flying out behind is not a flag, it is a curtain. That other thing up there is the sun, but I didn't get enough distance on it. I do not remember, now, what that thing is that is in front of the man who is running, but I think it is a haystack or a woman. This study was exhibited in the Paris Salon of 1879, but did not take any medal; they do not give medals for studies.

We discharged the carriage at the bridge. The river was full of logs—long, slender, barkless pine logs—and we leaned on the rails of the bridge, and watched the men put them together into rafts. These rafts were of a shape and construction to suit the crookedness and extreme narrowness of the Neckar. They were from fifty to one hundred yards long, and they gradually tapered from a nine-log breadth at their sterns, to a three-log breadth at their bow-ends. The main part of the steering is done at the bow, with a pole; the three-log breadth there furnishes room for only the steersman, for these little logs are not larger around than an average young lady's waist. The connections of the several sections of the raft are slack and pliant, so that the raft may be readily bent into any sort of curve required by the shape of the river.

The Neckar is in many places so narrow that a person can throw a dog across it, if he has one; when it is also sharply curved in such places, the raftsman has to do some pretty nice snug piloting to make the turns. The river is not always allowed to spread over its whole bed—which is as much as thirty, and sometimes forty yards wide—but is split into three equal bodies of water, by stone dikes which throw the main volume, depth, and current into the central one. In low water these neat narrow-edged dikes project four or five inches above the surface, like the comb of a submerged roof, but in high water they are overflowed. A hatful of rain makes high water in the Neckar, and a basketful produces an overflow.

There are dikes abreast the Schloss Hotel, and the current is violently swift at that point. I used to sit for hours in my glass cage, watching the long, narrow rafts slip along through the central channel, grazing the right-bank dike and aiming carefully for the middle arch of the stone bridge below; I watched them in this way, and lost all this time hoping to see one of them hit the bridge-pier and wreck itself sometime or other, but was always disappointed. One was smashed there one morning, but I had just stepped into my room a moment to light a pipe, so I lost it.

While I was looking down upon the rafts that morning in Heilbronn, the daredevil spirit of adventure came suddenly upon me, and I said to my comrades:

"*I* am going to Heidelberg on a raft. Will you venture with me?"

Their faces paled a little, but they assented with as good a grace as they could. Harris wanted to cable his mother—thought it his duty to do that, as he was all she had in this world—so, while he attended to this, I went down to the longest and finest raft and hailed the captain with a hearty "Ahoy, shipmate!" which put us upon pleasant terms at once, and we entered upon business. I said we were on a pedestrian tour to Heidelberg, and would like to take passage with him. I said this partly through young Z, who spoke German very well, and partly through Mr. X, who spoke it peculiarly. I can *understand* German as well as the maniac that invented it, but I *talk* it best through an interpreter.

The captain hitched up his trousers, then shifted his quid thoughtfully. Presently he said just what I was expecting he would say—that he had no license to carry passengers, and therefore was afraid the law would be after him in case the matter got noised about or any accident happened. So I *chartered* the raft and the crew and took all the responsibilities on myself.

With a rattling song the starboard watch bent to their work and hove the cable short, then got the anchor home, and our bark moved off with a stately stride, and soon was bowling along at about two knots an hour.

Our party were grouped amidships. At first the talk was a little gloomy, and ran mainly upon the shortness of life, the uncertainty of it, the perils which beset it, and the need and wisdom of being always prepared for the worst; this shaded off into low-voiced references to the dangers of the deep, and kindred matters; but as the gray east began to redden and the mysterious solemnity and silence of the dawn to give place to the joy-songs of the birds, the talk took a cheerier tone, and our spirits began to rise steadily.

Germany, in the summer, is the perfection of the beautiful, but nobody has understood, and realized, and enjoyed the utmost possibilities of this soft and peaceful beauty unless he has voyaged down the Neckar on a raft. The motion of a raft is the needful motion; it is gentle, and gliding, and smooth, and noiseless; it calms down all feverish activities, it soothes to sleep all nervous hurry and impatience; under its restful influence all the troubles and vexations and sorrows that harass the mind vanish away, and existence becomes a dream, a charm, a deep and tranquil ecstasy. How it contrasts with hot and perspiring pedestrianism, and dusty and deafening railroad rush, and tedious jolting behind tired horses over blinding white roads!

We went slipping silently along, between the green

and fragrant banks, with a sense of pleasure and contentment that grew, and grew, all the time. Sometimes the banks were overhung with thick masses of willows that wholly hid the ground behind; sometimes we had noble hills on one hand, clothed densely with foliage to their tops, and on the other hand open levels blazing with poppies, or clothed in the rich blue of the corn-flower; sometimes we drifted in the shadow of forests, and sometimes along the margin of long stretches of velvety grass, fresh and green and bright, a tireless charm to the eye. And the birds!—they were everywhere; they swept back and forth across the river constantly, and their jubilant music was never stilled.

It was a deep and satisfying pleasure to see the sun create the new morning, and gradually, patiently, lovingly, clothe it on with splendor after splendor, and glory after glory, till the miracle was complete. How different is this marvel observed from a raft, from what it is when one observes it through the dingy windows of a railway-station in some wretched village while he munches a petrified sandwich and waits for the train.

CHAPTER XV

DOWN THE RIVER

MEN and women and cattle were at work in the dewy fields by this time. The people often stepped aboard the raft, as we glided along the grassy shores, and gossiped with us and with the crew for a hundred yards or so, then stepped ashore again, refreshed by the ride.

Only the men did this; the women were too busy. The women do all kinds of work on the continent. They dig, they hoe, they reap, they sow, they bear monstrous burdens on their backs, they shove similar ones long distances on wheelbarrows, they drag the cart when there is no dog or lean cow to drag it—and when there is, they assist the dog or cow. Age is no matter—the older the woman the stronger she is, apparently. On the farm a woman's duties are not defined—she does a little of everything; but in the towns it is different, there she only does certain things, the men do the rest. For instance, a hotel chambermaid has nothing to do but make beds and fires in fifty or sixty rooms, bring towels and candles, and fetch several tons of water up several flights of stairs, a hundred pounds at a time, in prodigious metal pitchers. She does not have to work more than eighteen or twenty hours a day, and she can always get down on her knees and scrub the floors of halls and closets when she is tired and needs a rest.

As the morning advanced and the weather grew hot, we took off our outside clothing and sat in a row along the edge of the raft and enjoyed the scenery, with our sun-umbrellas over our heads and our legs dangling in the water. Every now and then we plunged in and had a swim. Every projecting grassy cape had its joyous group of naked children, the boys to themselves and the girls to themselves, the latter usually in care of some motherly dame who sat in the shade of a tree with her knitting. The little boys swam out to us, sometimes, but the little maids stood knee-deep in the water and stopped their splashing and frolicking to inspect the raft with their innocent eyes as it drifted by. Once we turned a corner suddenly and surprised a slender girl of twelve years or upward, just stepping into the water. She had not time to run, but she did what answered just as well; she promptly drew a lithe young willow bough athwart her white body with one hand, and then contemplated us with a simple and untroubled interest. Thus she stood while we glided by. She was a pretty creature, and she and her willow bough made a very pretty picture, and one which could not offend the modesty of the most fastidious spectator. Her white skin had a low bank of fresh green willows for background and effective contrast—for she stood against them—and above and out of them projected the eager faces and white shoulders of two smaller girls.

Toward noon we heard the inspiriting cry:
"Sail ho!"
"Where away?" shouted the captain.
"Three points off the weather bow!"
We ran forward to see the vessel. It proved to
be a steamboat—for they had begun to run a
steamer up the Neckar, for the first time in May.
She was a tug, and one of very peculiar build and
aspect. I had often watched her from the hotel,
and wondered how she propelled herself, for apparently she had no propeller or paddles. She came
churning along, now, making a deal of noise of one
kind and another, and aggravating it every now and
then by blowing a hoarse whistle. She had nine
keel-boats hitched on behind and following after her
in a long, slender rank. We met her in a narrow
place, between dikes, and there was hardly room for
us both in the cramped passage. As she went
grinding and groaning by, we perceived the secret of
her moving impulse. She did not drive herself up
the river with paddles or propeller, she pulled herself by hauling on a great chain. This chain is laid
in the bed of the river and is only fastened at the
two ends. It is seventy miles long. It comes in
over the boat's bow, passes around a drum, and is
payed out astern. She pulls on that chain, and so
drags herself up the river or down it. She has
neither bow nor stern, strictly speaking, for she has
a long-bladed rudder on each end and she never
turns around. She uses both rudders all the time,
and they are powerful enough to enable her to turn
to the right or the left and steer around curves, in

MARK TWAIN

spite of the strong resistance of the chain. I would not have believed that that impossible thing could be done; but I saw it done, and therefore I know that there is one impossible thing which *can* be done. What miracle will man attempt next?

We met many big keel-boats on their way up, using sails, mule power, and profanity—a tedious and laborious business. A wire rope led from the foretopmast to the file of mules on the tow-path a hundred yards ahead, and by dint of much banging and swearing and urging, the detachment of drivers managed to get a speed of two or three miles an hour out of the mules against the stiff current. The Neckar has always been used as a canal, and thus has given employment to a great many men and animals; but now that this steamboat is able, with a small crew and a bushel or so of coal, to take nine keel-boats farther up the river in one hour than thirty men and thirty mules can do it in two, it is believed that the old-fashioned towing industry is on its death-bed. A second steamboat began work in the Neckar three months after the first one was put in service.

At noon we stepped ashore and bought some bottled beer and got some chickens cooked, while the raft waited; then we immediately put to sea again, and had our dinner while the beer was cold and the chickens hot. There is no pleasanter place for such a meal than a raft that is gliding down the winding Neckar past green meadows and wooded hills, and slumbering villages, and craggy heights graced with crumbling towers and battlements.

In one place we saw a nicely dressed German gentleman without any spectacles. Before I could come to anchor he had got away. It was a great pity. I so wanted to make a sketch of him. The captain comforted me for my loss, however, by saying that the man was without any doubt a fraud who had spectacles, but kept them in his pocket in order to make himself conspicuous.

Below Hassmersheim we passed Hornberg, Götz von Berlichingen's old castle. It stands on a bold elevation two hundred feet above the surface of the river; it has high vine-clad walls inclosing trees, and a peaked tower about seventy-five feet high. The steep hillside, from the castle clear down to the water's edge, is terraced, and clothed thick with grape vines. This is like farming a mansard roof. All the steeps along that part of the river which furnish the proper exposure, are given up to the grape. That region is a great producer of Rhine wines. The Germans are exceedingly fond of Rhine wines; they are put up in tall, slender bottles, and are considered a pleasant beverage. One tells them from vinegar by the label.

The Hornberg hill is to be tunneled, and the new railway will pass under the castle.

THE CAVE OF THE SPECTER

Two miles below Hornberg castle is a cave in a low cliff, which the captain of the raft said had once been occupied by a beautiful heiress of Hornberg— the Lady Gertrude—in the old times. It was seven hundred years ago. She had a number of rich and noble lovers and one poor and obscure one, Sir Wendel Lobenfeld. With the native chuckleheadedness of the heroine of romance, she preferred the poor and obscure lover. With the native sound judgment of the father of a heroine of romance, the von Berlichingen of that day shut his daughter up in his donjon keep, or his oubliette, or his culverin, or some such place, and resolved that she should stay there until she selected a husband from among her rich and noble lovers. The latter visited her and persecuted her with their supplications, but without effect, for her heart was true to her poor despised Crusader, who was fighting in the Holy Land. Finally, she resolved that she would endure the attentions of the rich lovers no longer; so one stormy night she escaped and went down the river and hid herself in the cave on the other side. Her father ransacked the country for her, but found not a trace of her. As the days went by, and still no tidings of her came, his conscience began to torture him, and he caused proclamation to be made that if she were yet living and would return, he would oppose her no longer, she might marry whom she would. The months dragged on, all hope forsook the old man, he ceased from his customary pursuits and pleasures, he devoted himself to pious works, and longed for the deliverance of death.

Now just at midnight, every night, the lost heiress stood in the mouth of her cave, arrayed in white robes, and sang a little love ballad which her Crusader had made for her. She judged that if he came home alive the superstitious peasants would tell him about the ghost that sang in the cave, and that as soon as they described the ballad he would know that none but he and she knew that song, therefore he would suspect that she was alive, and would come and find her. As time went on, the people of the region became sorely distressed about the Specter of the Haunted Cave. It was said that ill luck of one kind or another always overtook any one who had the misfortune to hear that song. Eventually, every calamity that happened thereabouts was laid at the door of that music. Consequently, no boatmen would consent to pass the cave at night; the peasants shunned the place, even in the daytime.

But the faithful girl sang on, night after night, month after month, and patiently waited; her reward must come at last. Five years dragged by, and still, every night at midnight, the plaintive tones floated out over the silent land, while the distant boatmen and peasants thrust their fingers into their ears and shuddered out a prayer.

And now came the Crusader home, bronzed and battle-scarred, but bringing a great and splendid fame to lay at the feet of his bride. The old lord of Hornberg received him as a son, and wanted him to stay by him and be the comfort and blessing of his age; but the tale of that young girl's devotion to him and its pathetic consequences made a changed man of the knight. He could not enjoy his well-earned rest. He said his heart was broken, he would give the remnant of his life to high deeds in the cause of humanity, and so find a worthy death and a blessed reunion with the brave true heart whose love had more honored him than all his victories in war.

When the people heard this resolve of his, they came and told him there was a pitiless dragon in human disguise in the Haunted Cave, a dread creature which no knight had yet been bold enough to face, and begged him to rid the land of its desolating presence. He said he would do it. They told him about the song, and when he asked what song it was, they said the memory of it was gone, for nobody had been hardy enough to listen to it for the past four years and more.

Toward midnight the Crusader came floating down the river in a boat, with his trusty cross-bow in his hands. He drifted silently through the dim reflections of the crags and trees, with his intent eyes fixed upon the low cliff which he was approaching. As he drew nearer, he discerned the black mouth of the cave. Now—is that a white figure? Yes. The plaintive song begins to well forth and float away over meadow and river—the cross-bow is slowly raised to position, a steady aim is taken, the bolt flies straight to the mark—the figure sinks down, still singing, the knight takes the wool out of his ears, and recognizes the old ballad—too late! Ah, if he had only not put the wool in his ears!

The Crusader went away to the wars again, and presently fell in battle, fighting for the Cross. Tradition says that during several centuries the spirit of the unfortunate girl sang nightly from the cave at midnight, but the music carried no curse

Bird waiting for a Fish, a
common Spectacle.
(Perspective of Bird not correct.)

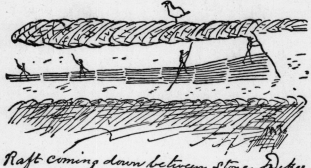

Raft coming down between Stone Dikes.

Raft curving itself through
crooked peece of River. (merely
a study, not a finished
picture)

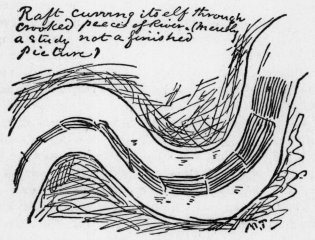

RAFTING ON THE NECKAR

with it; and although many listened for the mysterious sounds, few were favored, since only those could hear them who had never failed in a trust. It is believed that the singing still continues, but it is known that nobody has heard it during the present century.

CHAPTER XVI

AN ANCIENT LEGEND OF THE RHINE

THE last legend reminds one of the "Lorelei"—
a legend of the Rhine. There is a song called
"The Lorelei."

Germany is rich in folk-songs, and the words and
airs of several of them are peculiarly beautiful—
but "The Lorelei" is the people's favorite. I
could not endure it at first, but by and by it began
to take hold of me, and now there is no tune which
I like so well.

It is not possible that it is much known in America,
else I should have heard it there. The fact that I
never heard it there, is evidence that there are
others in my country who have fared likewise;
therefore, for the sake of these, I mean to print the
words and the music in this chapter. And I will
refresh the reader's memory by printing the legend
of the Lorelei, too. I have it by me in the *Legends
of the Rhine*, done into English by the wildly
gifted Garnham, Bachelor of Arts. I print the legend
partly to refresh my own memory, too, for I have
never read it before.

THE LEGEND

Lore (two syllables) was a water nymph who
used to sit on a high rock called Ley or Lei (pro-

nounced like our word *lie*) in the Rhine, and lure boatmen to destruction in a furious rapid which marred the channel at that spot. She so bewitched them with her plaintive songs and her wonderful beauty that they forgot everything else to gaze up at her, and so they presently drifted among the broken reefs and were lost.

In those old, old times, the Count Bruno lived in a great castle near there with his son, the Count Hermann, a youth of twenty. Hermann had heard a great deal about the beautiful Lore, and had finally fallen very deeply in love with her without having seen her. So he used to wander to the neighborhood of the Lei, evenings, with his Zither and "Express his Longing in low Singing," as Garnham says. On one of these occasions, "suddenly there hovered around the top of the rock a brightness of unequaled clearness and color, which, in increasingly smaller circles thickened, was the enchanting figure of the beautiful Lore.

"An unintentional cry of Joy escaped the Youth, he let his Zither fall, and with extended arms he called out the name of the enigmatical Being, who seemed to stoop lovingly to him and beckon to him in a friendly manner; indeed, if his ear did not deceive him, she called his name with unutterable sweet Whispers, proper to love. Beside himself with delight the youth lost his Senses and sank senseless to the earth."

After that he was a changed person. He went dreaming about, thinking only of his fairy and caring for naught else in the world. "The old count

saw with affliction this changement in his son,"
whose cause he could not divine, and tried to di-
vert his mind into cheerful channels, but to no
purpose. Then the old count used authority. He
commanded the youth to betake himself to the
camp. Obedience was promised. Garnham says:

"It was on the evening before his departure, as
he wished still once to visit the Lei and offer to the
Nymph of the Rhine his Sighs, the tones of his
Zither, and his Songs. He went, in his boat, this
time accompanied by a faithful squire, down the
stream. The moon shed her silvery light over the
whole country; the steep bank mountains appeared
in the most fantastical shapes, and the high oaks on
either side bowed their Branches on Hermann's
passing. As soon as he approached the Lei, and
was aware of the surf-waves, his attendant was
seized with an inexpressible Anxiety and he begged
permission to land; but the Knight swept the strings
of his Guitar and sang:

"Once I saw thee in dark night,
  In supernatural Beauty bright;
Of Light-rays, was the Figure wove,
  To share its light, locked-hair strove.

"Thy Garment color wave-dove,
  By thy hand the sign of love,
Thy eyes sweet enchantment,
  Raying to me, oh! entrancement.

"O, wert thou but my sweetheart,
  How willingly thy love to part!
With delight I should be bound
  To thy rocky house in deep ground."

That Hermann should have gone to that place at all, was not wise; that he should have gone with such a song as that in his mouth was a most serious mistake. The Lorelei did not "call his name in unutterable sweet Whispers" this time. No, that song naturally worked an instant and thorough "changement" in her; and not only that, but it stirred the bowels of the whole afflicted region round about there—for—

"Scarcely had these tones sounded, everywhere there began tumult and sound, as if voices above and below the water. On the Lei rose flames, the Fairy stood above, as that time, and beckoned with her right hand clearly and urgently to the infatuated Knight, while with a staff in her left she called the waves to her service. They began to mount heavenward; the boat was upset, mocking every exertion; the waves rose to the gunwale, and splitting on the hard stones, the Boat broke into Pieces. The youth sank into the depths, but the squire was thrown on shore by a powerful wave."

The bitterest things have been said about the Lorelei during many centuries, but surely her conduct upon this occasion entitles her to our respect. One feels drawn tenderly toward her and is moved to forget her many crimes and remember only the good deed that crowned and closed her career.

"The Fairy was never more seen; but her enchanting tones have often been heard. In the beautiful, refreshing, still nights of spring, when the moon pours her silver light over the Country, the listening shipper hears from the rushing of the waves, the echoing Clang of a wonderfully charming voice, which sings a song from the crystal castle, and with sorrow and fear he thinks on the young Count Hermann, seduced by the Nymph."

Here is the music, and the German words by Heinrich Heine. This song has been a favorite in Germany for forty years, and will remain a favorite always, maybe (see pp. 124–125).

I have a prejudice against people who print things in a foreign language and add no translation. When I am the reader, and the author considers me able to do the translating myself, he pays me quite a nice compliment—but if he would do the translating for me I would try to get along without the compliment.

If I were at home, no doubt I could get a translation of this poem, but I am abroad and can't; therefore I will make a translation myself. It may not be a good one, for poetry is out of my line, but it will serve my purpose—which is, to give the un-German young girl a jingle of words to hang the tune on until she can get hold of a good version, made by some one who is a poet and knows how to convey a poetical thought from one language to another.

THE LORELEI

I cannot divine what it meaneth,
This haunting nameless pain:
A tale of the bygone ages
Keeps brooding through my brain:

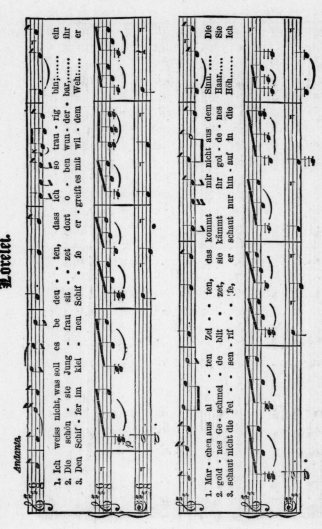

Lorelei.

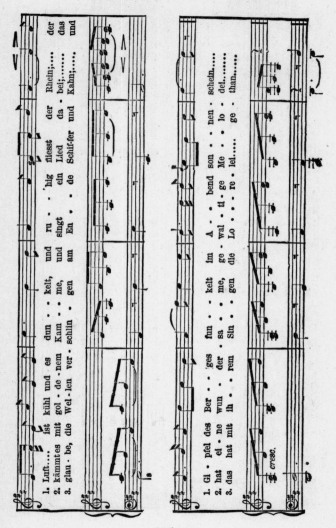

MARK TWAIN

The faint air cools in the gloaming,
  And peaceful flows the Rhine,
The thirsty summits are drinking
  The sunset's flooding wine;

The loveliest maiden is sitting
  High-throned in yon blue air,
Her golden jewels are shining,
  She combs her golden hair;

She combs with a comb that is golden,
  And sings a weird refrain
That steeps in a deadly enchantment
  The list'ner's ravished brain:

The doomed in his drifting shallop,
  Is tranced with the sad sweet tone,
He sees not the yawning breakers,
  He sees but the maid alone:

The pitiless billows engulf him!—
  So perish sailor and bark;
And this, with her baleful singing,
  Is the Lorelei's grewsome work.

I have a translation by Garnham, Bachelor of
Arts, in the *Legends of the Rhine*, but it would
not answer the purpose I mentioned above, because
the measure is too nobly irregular; it don't fit the
tune snugly enough; in places it hangs over at
the ends too far, and in other places one runs
out of words before he gets to the end of a bar.
Still, Garnham's translation has high merits, and
I am not dreaming of leaving it out of my book.
I believe this poet is wholly unknown in America
and England; I take peculiar pleasure in bringing

him forward because I consider that I discovered him:

THE LORELEI

Translated by L. W. Garnham, B.A.

I do not know what it signifies.
  That I am so sorrowful?
A fable of old Times so terrifies,
  Leaves my heart so thoughtful.

The air is cool and it darkens,
  And calmly flows the Rhine;
The summit of the mountain hearkens
  In evening sunshine line.

The most beautiful Maiden entrances
  Above wonderfully there,
Her beautiful golden attire glances,
  She combs her golden hair.

With golden comb so lustrous,
  And thereby a song sings,
It has a tone so wondrous,
  That powerful melody rings.

The shipper in the little ship
  It effects with woes sad might;
He does not see the rocky clip,
  He only regards dreaded height.

I believe the turbulent waves
  Swallow at last shipper and boat;
She with her singing craves
  All to visit her magic moat.

No translation could be closer. He has got in all the facts; and in their regular order, too. There is not a statistic wanting. It is as succinct as an invoice. That is what a translation ought to be; it

should exactly reflect the thought of the original.
You can't *sing* "Above wonderfully there," because
it simply won't go to the tune, without damaging
the singer; but it is a most clingingly exact translation of *Dort oben wunderbar*—fits it like a blister.
Mr. Garnham's reproduction has other merits—a
hundred of them—but it is not necessary to point
them out.   They will be detected.

No one with a specialty can hope to have a
monopoly of it.   Even Garnham has a rival.   Mr.
X had a small pamphlet with him which he had
bought while on a visit to Munich.   It was entitled
A Catalogue of Pictures in the Old Pinacotek, and was
written in a peculiar kind of English.   Here are a few
extracts:

"It is not permitted to make use of the work in
question to a publication of the same contents as
well as to the pirated edition of it."

"An evening landscape.   In the foreground near
a pond and a group of white beeches is leading a
footpath animated by travelers."

"A learned man in a cynical and torn dress holding an open book in his hand."

"St. Bartholomew and the Executioner with the
knife to fulfil the martyr."

"Portrait of a young man.   A long while this
picture was thought to be Bindi Altoviti's portrait;
now somebody will again have it to be the self-
portrait of Raphael."

"Susan bathing, surprised by the two old man.
In the background the lapidation of the con-
demned."

("Lapidation" is good; it is much more elegant than "stoning.")

"St. Rochus sitting in a landscape with an angel who looks at his plague-sore, whilst the dog the bread in his mouth attents him."

"Spring. The Goddess Flora, sitting. Behind her a fertile valley perfused by a river."

"A beautiful bouquet animated by May-bugs, etc."

"A warrior in armor with a gypseous pipe in his hand leans against a table and blows the smoke far away of himself."

"A Dutch landscape along a navigable river which perfuses it till to the background."

"Some peasants singing in a cottage. A woman lets drink a child out of a cup."

"St. John's head as a boy—painted in fresco on a brick." (Meaning a tile.)

"A young man of the Riccio family, his hair cut off right at the end, dressed in black with the same cap. Attributed to Raphael, but the signation is false."

"The Virgin holding the Infant. It is very painted in the manner of Sassoferrato."

"A Larder with greens and dead game animated by a cook-maid and two kitchen-boys."

However, the English of this catalogue is at least as happy as that which distinguishes an inscription upon a certain picture in Rome—to wit:

"Revelations - View. St. John in Patterson's Island."

But meantime the raft is moving on.

CHAPTER XVII

A MILE or two above Eberbach we saw a peculiar ruin projecting above the foliage which clothed the peak of a high and very steep hill. This ruin consisted of merely a couple of crumbling masses of masonry which bore a rude resemblance to human faces; they leaned forward and touched foreheads, and had the look of being absorbed in conversation. This ruin had nothing very imposing or picturesque about it, and there was no great deal of it, yet it was called the "Spectacular Ruin."

LEGEND OF THE "SPECTACULAR RUIN"

The captain of the raft, who was as full of history as he could stick, said that in the Middle Ages a most prodigious fire-breathing dragon used to live in that region, and made more trouble than a tax-collector. He was as long as a railway-train, and had the customary impenetrable green scales all over him. His breath bred pestilence and conflagration, and his appetite bred famine. He ate men and cattle impartially, and was exceedingly unpopular. The German emperor of that day made the usual offer: he would grant to the destroyer of the dragon, any one solitary thing he might ask for; for he had a surplusage of daughters, and it was customary for dragon-killers to take a daughter for pay.

So the most renowned knights came from the four corners of the earth and retired down the dragon's throat one after the other. A panic arose and spread. Heroes grew cautious. The procession ceased. The dragon became more destructive than ever. The people lost all hope of succor, and fled to the mountains for refuge.

At last Sir Wissenschaft, a poor and obscure knight, out of a far country, arrived to do battle with the monster. A pitiable object he was, with his armor hanging in rags about him, and his strange-shaped knapsack strapped upon his back. Everybody turned up their noses at him, and some openly jeered him. But he was calm. He simply inquired if the emperor's offer was still in force. The emperor said it was — but charitably advised him to go and hunt hares and not endanger so precious a life as his in an attempt which had brought death to so many of the world's most illustrious heroes.

But this tramp only asked—"Were any of these heroes men of science?" This raised a laugh, of course, for science was despised in those days. But the tramp was not in the least ruffled. He said he might be a little in advance of his age, but no matter—science would come to be honored, some time or other. He said he would march against the dragon in the morning. Out of compassion, then, a decent spear was offered him, but he declined, and said, "spears were useless to men of science." They allowed him to sup in the servants' hall, and gave him a bed in the stables.

When he started forth in the morning, thousands were gathered to see. The emperor said:

"Do not be rash, take a spear, and leave off your knapsack."

But the tramp said:

"It is not a knapsack," and moved straight on.

The dragon was waiting and ready. He was breathing forth vast volumes of sulphurous smoke and lurid blasts of flame. The ragged knight stole warily to a good position, then he unslung his cylindrical knapsack—which was simply the common fire-extinguisher known to modern times—and the first chance he got he turned on his hose and shot the dragon square in the center of his cavernous mouth. Out went the fires in an instant, and the dragon curled up and died.

This man had brought brains to his aid. He had reared dragons from the egg, in his laboratory, he had watched over them like a mother, and patiently studied them and experimented upon them while they grew. Thus he had found out that fire was the life principle of a dragon; put out the dragon's fires and it could make steam no longer, and must die. He could not put out a fire with a spear, therefore he invented the extinguisher. The dragon being dead, the emperor fell on the hero's neck and said:

"Deliverer, name your request," at the same time beckoning out behind with his heel for a detachment of his daughters to form and advance. But the tramp gave them no observance. He simply said:

"My request is, that upon me be conferred the monopoly of the manufacture and sale of spectacles in Germany."

The emperor sprang aside and exclaimed:

"This transcends all the impudence I ever heard! A modest demand, by my halidome! Why didn't you ask for the imperial revenues at once, and be done with it?"

But the monarch had given his word, and he kept it. To everybody's surprise, the unselfish monopolist immediately reduced the price of spectacles to such a degree that a great and crushing burden was removed from the nation. The emperor, to commemorate this generous act, and to testify his appreciation of it, issued a decree commanding everybody to buy this benefactor's spectacles and wear them, whether they needed them or not.

So originated the wide-spread custom of wearing spectacles in Germany; and as a custom once established in these old lands is imperishable, this one remains universal in the empire to this day. Such is the legend of the monopolist's once stately and sumptuous castle, now called the "Spectacular Ruin."

On the right bank, two or three miles below the Spectacular Ruin, we passed by a noble pile of castellated buildings overlooking the water from the crest of a lofty elevation. A stretch of two hundred yards of the high front wall was heavily draped with ivy, and out of the mass of buildings within rose three picturesque old towers. The place was in fine order, and was inhabited by a family of princely rank. This castle had its legend, too, but I should not feel justified in repeating it because I doubted the truth of some of its minor details.

Along in this region a multitude of Italian laborers were blasting away the frontage of the hills to make room for the new railway. They were fifty or a hundred feet above the river. As we turned a sharp corner they began to wave signals and shout warnings to us to look out for the explosions. It was all very well to warn us, but what could *we* do? You can't back a raft up-stream, you can't hurry it down-stream, you can't scatter out to one side when you haven't any room to speak of, you won't take to the perpendicular cliffs on the other shore when they appear to be blasting there, too. Your resources are limited, you see. There is simply nothing for it but to watch and pray.

For some hours we had been making three and a half or four miles an hour and we were still making that. We had been dancing right along until those men began to shout; then for the next ten minutes it seemed to me that I had never seen a raft go so slowly. When the first blast went off we raised our sun-umbrellas and waited for the result. No harm done; none of the stones fell in the water. Another blast followed, and another and another. Some of the rubbish fell in the water just astern of us.

We ran that whole battery of nine blasts in a row, and it was certainly one of the most exciting and uncomfortable weeks I ever spent, either aship or ashore. Of course we frequently manned the poles and shoved earnestly for a second or so, but every

time one of those spurts of dust and debris shot aloft
every man dropped his pole and looked up to get
the bearings of his share of it. It was very busy
times along there for a while. It appeared certain
that we must perish, but even that was not the
bitterest thought; no, the abjectly unheroic nature
of the death—that was the sting—that and the
bizarre wording of the resulting obituary: "*Shot
with a rock, on a raft.*" There would be no poetry
written about it. None *could* be written about it.
Example:

> *Not* by war's shock, or war's shaft,—
> *Shot*, with a rock, on a raft.

No poet who valued his reputation would touch
such a theme as that. I should be distinguished as
the only "distinguished dead" who went down to
the grave unsonneted, in 1878.

But we escaped, and I have never regretted it.
The last blast was a peculiarly strong one, and after
the small rubbish was done raining around us and we
were just going to shake hands over our deliverance,
a later and larger stone came down amongst our
little group of pedestrians and wrecked an umbrella.
It did no other harm, but we took to the water just
the same.

It seems that the heavy work in the quarries and
the new railway gradings is done mainly by Italians.
That was a revelation. We have the notion in our
country that Italians never do heavy work at all, but
confine themselves to the lighter arts, like organ-
grinding, operatic singing, and assassination. We
have blundered, that is plain.

All along the river, near every village, we saw little station-houses for the future railway. They were finished and waiting for the rails and business. They were as trim and snug and pretty as they could be. They were always of brick or stone; they were of graceful shape, they had vines and flowers about them already, and around them the grass was bright and green, and showed that it was carefully looked after. They were a decoration to the beautiful landscape, not an offense. Wherever one saw a pile of gravel or a pile of broken stone, it was always heaped as trimly and exactly as a new grave or a stack of cannon-balls; nothing about those stations or along the railroad or the wagon-road was allowed to look shabby or be unornamental. The keeping a country in such beautiful order as Germany exhibits, has a wise practical side to it, too, for it keeps thousands of people in work and bread who would otherwise be idle and mischievous.

As the night shut down, the captain wanted to tie up, but I thought maybe we might make Hirschhorn, so we went on. Presently the sky became overcast, and the captain came aft looking uneasy. He cast his eye aloft, then shook his head, and said it was coming on to blow. My party wanted to land at once—therefore I wanted to go on. The captain said we ought to shorten sail anyway, out of common prudence. Consequently, the larboard watch was ordered to lay in his pole. It grew quite dark, now, and the wind began to rise. It wailed through the swaying branches of the trees, and swept our decks in fitful gusts. Things were taking on an ugly look. The captain shouted to the steersman on the forward log:

"How's she heading?"

The answer came faint and hoarse from far forward:

"Nor'-east-and-by-nor' — east-by-east, half-east, sir."

"Let her go off a point!"

"Aye-aye, sir!"

"What water have you got?"

"Shoal, sir. Two foot large, on the stabboard, two and a half scant on the labboard!"

"Let her go off another point!"

"Aye-aye, sir!"

"Forward, men, all of you! Lively, now! Stand by to crowd her round the weather corner!"

"Aye-aye, sir!"

Then followed a wild running and trampling and hoarse shouting, but the forms of the men were lost in the darkness and the sounds were distorted and confused by the roaring of the wind through the shingle-bundles. By this time the sea was running inches high, and threatening every moment to engulf the frail bark. Now came the mate, hurrying aft, and said, close to the captain's ear, in a low, agitated voice:

"Prepare for the worst, sir—we have sprung a leak!"

"Heavens! where?"

"Right aft the second row of logs."

"Nothing but a miracle can save us! Don't let the men know, or there will be a panic and mutiny!

Lay her in shore and stand by to jump with the stern-line the moment she touches. Gentlemen, I must look to you to second my endeavors in this hour of peril. You have hats—go forward and bail for your lives!"

Down swept another mighty blast of wind, clothed in spray and thick darkness. At such a moment as this, came from away forward that most appalling of all cries that are ever heard at sea:

"*Man overboard!*"

The captain shouted:

"Hard a-port! Never mind the man! Let him climb aboard or wade ashore!"

Another cry came down the wind:

"Breakers ahead!"

"Where away?"

"Not a log's length off her port fore-foot!"

We had groped our slippery way forward, and were now bailing with the frenzy of despair, when we heard the mate's terrified cry, from far aft:

"Stop that dashed bailing, or we shall be aground!"

But this was immediately followed by the glad shout:

"Land aboard the starboard transom!"

"Saved!" cried the captain. "Jump ashore and take a turn around a tree and pass the bight aboard!"

The next moment we were all on shore weeping and embracing for joy, while the rain poured down in torrents. The captain said he had been a mariner for forty years on the Neckar, and in that time had seen storms to make a man's cheek blanch and his pulses stop, but he had never, never seen a storm that even approached this one. How familiar that sounded! For I have been at sea a good deal and have heard that remark from captains with a frequency accordingly.

We framed in our minds the usual resolution of thanks and admiration and gratitude, and took the first opportunity to vote it, and put it in writing and present it to the captain, with the customary speech.

We tramped through the darkness and the drenching summer rain full three miles, and reached "The Naturalist Tavern" in the village of Hirschhorn just an hour before midnight, almost exhausted from hardship, fatigue, and terror. I can never forget that night.

The landlord was rich, and therefore could afford to be crusty and disobliging; he did not at all like being turned out of his warm bed to open his house for us. But no matter, his household got up and cooked a quick supper for us, and we brewed a hot punch for ourselves, to keep off consumption. After supper and punch we had an hour's soothing smoke while we fought the naval battle over again and voted the resolutions; then we retired to exceedingly neat and pretty chambers up-stairs that had clean, comfortable beds in them with heirloom pillow-cases most elaborately and tastefully embroidered by hand.

Such rooms and beds and embroidered linen are as frequent in German village inns as they are rare in ours. Our villages are superior to German villages in more merits, excellences, conveniences, and privileges than I can enumerate, but the hotels do not belong in the list.

"The Naturalist Tavern" was not a meaningless name; for all the halls and all the rooms were lined with large glass cases which were filled with all sorts of birds and animals, glass-eyed, ably stuffed, and set up in the most natural and eloquent and dramatic attitudes. The moment we were abed, the rain cleared away and the moon came out. I dozed off to sleep while contemplating a great white stuffed owl which was looking intently down on me from a high perch with the air of a person who thought he had met me before, but could not make out for certain.

But young Z did not get off so easily. He said that as he was sinking deliciously to sleep, the moon lifted away the shadows and developed a huge cat, on a bracket, dead and stuffed, but crouching, with every muscle tense, for a spring, and with its glittering glass eyes aimed straight at him. It made Z uncomfortable. He tried closing his own eyes, but that did not answer, for a natural instinct kept making him open them again to see if the cat was still getting ready to launch at him—which she always was. He tried turning his back, but that was a failure; he knew the sinister eyes were on him still. So at last he had to get up, after an hour or two of worry and experiment, and set the cat out in the hall. So he won, that time.

CHAPTER XVIII

IN the morning we took breakfast in the garden, under the trees, in the delightful German summer fashion. The air was filled with the fragrance of flowers and wild animals; the living portion of the menagerie of the "Naturalist Tavern" was all about us. There were great cages populous with fluttering and chattering foreign birds, and other great cages and greater wire pens, populous with quadrupeds, both native and foreign. There were some free creatures, too, and quite sociable ones they were. White rabbits went loping about the place, and occasionally came and sniffed at our shoes and shins; a fawn, with a red ribbon on its neck, walked up and examined us fearlessly; rare breeds of chickens and doves begged for crumbs, and a poor old tailless raven hopped about with a humble, shamefaced mien which said, "Please do not notice my exposure—think how you would feel in my circumstances, and be charitable." If he was observed too much, he would retire behind something and stay there until he judged the party's interest had found another object. I never have seen another dumb creature that was so morbidly sensitive. Bayard Taylor, who could interpret the dim reasonings of animals, and understood their moral natures better than most men, would have found some way to make this poor old chap forget his troubles for a while, but we have not his kindly art, and so had to leave the raven to his griefs.

After breakfast we climbed the hill and visited the ancient castle of Hirschhorn, and the ruined church near it. There were some curious old bas-reliefs leaning against the inner walls of the church— sculptured lords of Hirschhorn in complete armor, and ladies of Hirschhorn in the picturesque court costumes of the Middle Ages. These things are suffering damage and passing to decay, for the last Hirschhorn has been dead two hundred years, and there is nobody now who cares to preserve the family relics. In the chancel was a twisted stone column, and the captain told us a legend about it, of course, for in the matter of legends he could not seem to restrain himself; but I do not repeat his tale because there was nothing plausible about it except that the Hero wrenched this column into its present screw-shape with his hands—just one single wrench. All the rest of the legend was doubtful.

But Hirschhorn is best seen from a distance, down the river. Then the clustered brown towers perched on the green hilltop, and the old battlemented stone wall, stretching up and over the grassy ridge and dis- appearing in the leafy sea beyond, make a picture whose grace and beauty entirely satisfy the eye.

We descended from the church by steep stone stairways which curved this way and that down narrow alleys between the packed and dirty tene- ments of the village. It was a quarter well stocked with deformed, leering, unkempt and uncombed idiots, who held out hands or caps and begged piteously. The people of the quarter were not all idiots, of course, but all that begged seemed to be, and were said to be.

I was thinking of going by skiff to the next town, Neckarsteinach; so I ran to the riverside in advance of the party and asked a man there if he had a boat to hire. I suppose I must have spoken High German—Court German—I intended it for that, anyway—so he did not understand me. I turned and twisted my question around and about, trying to strike that man's average, but failed. He could not make out what I wanted. Now Mr. X arrived, faced this same man, looked him in the eye, and emptied this sentence on him, in the most glib and confident way:

"Can man boat get here?"

The mariner promptly understood and promptly answered. I can comprehend why he was able to understand that particular sentence, because by mere accident all the words in it except "get" have the same sound and the same meaning in German that they have in English; but how he managed to understand Mr. X's next remark puzzled me. I will insert it, presently. X turned away a moment, and I asked the mariner if he could not find a board, and so construct an additional seat. I spoke in the purest German, but I might as well have spoken in the purest Choctaw for all the good it did. The man tried his best to understand me; he tried, and kept on trying, harder and harder, until I saw it was really of no use, and said:

"There, don't strain yourself—it is of no consequence."

Then X turned to him and crisply said:

"*Machen Sie* a flat board."

I wish my epitaph may tell the truth about me if the man did not answer up at once, and say he would go and borrow a board as soon as he had lit the pipe which he was filling.

We changed our mind about taking a boat, so we did not have to go. I have given Mr. X's two remarks just as he made them. Four of the five words in the first one were English, and that they were also German was only accidental, not intentional; three out of the five words in the second remark were English, and English only, and the two German ones did not mean anything in particular, in such a connection.

X always spoke English, to Germans, but his plan was to turn the sentence wrong end first and upside down, according to German construction, and sprinkle in a German word without any essential meaning to it, here and there, by way of flavor. Yet he always made himself understood. He could make those dialect-speaking raftsmen understand him, sometimes, when even young Z had failed with them; and young Z was a pretty good German scholar. For one thing, X always spoke with such confidence—perhaps that helped. And possibly the raftsmen's dialect was what is called *platt-Deutsch*, and so they found his English more familiar to their ears than another man's German. Quite indifferent students of German can read Fritz Reuter's charming platt-Deutsch tales with some little facility because many of the words are English. I suppose this is the tongue which our Saxon ancestors carried to England with them. By and by I will inquire of some other philologist.

However, in the mean time it had transpired that the men employed to calk the raft had found that the leak was not a leak at all, but only a crack between the logs—a crack which belonged there, and was not dangerous, but had been magnified into a leak by the disordered imagination of the mate. Therefore we went aboard again with a good degree of confidence, and presently got to sea without accident. As we swam smoothly along between the enchanting shores, we fell to swapping notes about manners and customs in Germany and elsewhere.

As I write, now, many months later, I perceive that each of us, by observing and noting and inquiring, diligently and day by day, had managed to lay in a most varied and opulent stock of misinformation. But this is not surprising; it is very difficult to get accurate details in any country.

For example, I had the idea, once, in Heidelberg, to find out all about those five student-corps. I started with the White Cap Corps. I began to inquire of this and that and the other citizen, and here is what I found out:

1. It is called the Prussian Corps, because none but Prussians are admitted to it.

2. It is called the Prussian Corps for no particular reason. It has simply pleased each corps to name itself after some German state.

3. It is not named the Prussian Corps at all, but only the White Cap Corps.

4. Any student can belong to it who is a German by birth.

5. Any student can belong to it who is European by birth.

6. Any European-born student can belong to it, except he be a Frenchman.

7. Any student can belong to it, no matter where he was born.

8. No student can belong to it who is not of noble blood.

9. No student can belong to it who cannot show three full generations of noble descent.

10. Nobility is not a necessary qualification.

11. No moneyless student can belong to it.

12. Money qualification is nonsense—such a thing has never been thought of.

'I got some of this information from students themselves—students who did not belong to the corps.

I finally went to headquarters—to the White Caps—where I would have gone in the first place if I had been acquainted. But even at headquarters I found difficulties; I perceived that there were things about the White Cap Corps which one member knew and another one didn't. It was natural; for very few members of any organization know *all* that can be known about it. I doubt if there is a man or a woman in Heidelberg who would not answer promptly and confidently three out of every five questions about the White Cap Corps which a stranger might ask; yet it is a very safe bet that two of the three answers would be incorrect every time.

There is one German custom which is universal— the bowing courteously to strangers when sitting down at table or rising up from it. This bow startles a stranger out of his self-possession, the first time it occurs, and he is likely to fall over a chair or something, in his embarrassment, but it pleases him, nevertheless. One soon learns to expect this bow and be on the lookout and ready to return it; but to learn to lead off and make the initial bow one's self is a difficult matter for a diffident man. One thinks, "If I rise to go, and tender my bow, and these ladies and gentlemen take it into their heads to ignore the custom of their nation, and not return it, how shall I feel, in case I survive to feel anything." Therefore he is afraid to venture. He sits out the dinner, and makes the strangers rise first and originate the bowing. A table d'hôte dinner is a tedious affair for a man who seldom touches anything after the three first courses; therefore I used to do some pretty dreary waiting because of my fears. It took me months to assure myself that those fears were groundless, but I did assure myself at last by experimenting diligently through my agent. I made Harris get up and bow and leave; invariably his bow was returned, then I got up and bowed myself and retired.

Thus my education proceeded easily and comfortably for me, but not for Harris. Three courses of a table d'hôte dinner were enough for me, but Harris preferred thirteen.

Even after I had acquired full confidence, and no longer needed the agent's help, I sometimes encountered difficulties. Once at Baden-Baden I nearly lost a train because I could not be sure that three young ladies opposite me at table were Germans, since I had not heard them speak; they might be American, they might be English, it was not safe to venture a bow; but just as I had got that far with my thought, one of them began a German remark, to my great relief and gratitude; and before she had got out her third word, our bows had been delivered and graciously returned, and we were off.

There is a friendly something about the German character which is very winning. When Harris and I were making a pedestrian tour through the Black Forest, we stopped at a little country inn for dinner one day; two young ladies and a young gentleman entered and sat down opposite us. They were pedestrians, too. Our knapsacks were strapped upon our backs, but they had a sturdy youth along to carry theirs for them. All parties were hungry, so there was no talking. By and by the usual bows were exchanged, and we separated.

As we sat at a late breakfast in the hotel at Allerheiligen, next morning, these young people entered and took places near us without observing us; but presently they saw us and at once bowed and smiled; not ceremoniously, but with the gratified look of people who have found acquaintances where they were expecting strangers. Then they spoke of the weather and the roads. We also spoke of the weather and the roads. Next, they said they had

had an enjoyable walk, notwithstanding the weather. We said that that had been our case, too. Then they said they had walked thirty English miles the day before, and asked how many we had walked. I could not lie, so I told Harris to do it. Harris told them we had made thirty English miles, too. That was true; we had "made" them, though we had had a little assistance here and there.

After breakfast they found us trying to blast some information out of the dumb hotel clerk about routes, and observing that we were not succeeding pretty well, they went and got their maps and things, and pointed out and explained our course so clearly that even a New York detective could have followed it. And when we started they spoke out a hearty good-by and wished us a pleasant journey. Perhaps they were more generous with us than they might have been with native wayfarers because we were a forlorn lot and in a strange land; I don't know; I only know it was lovely to be treated so.

Very well, I took an American young lady to one of the fine balls in Baden-Baden, one night, and at the entrance-door up-stairs we were halted by an official—something about Miss Jones's dress was not according to rule; I don't remember what it was, now; something was wanting—her back hair, or a shawl, or a fan, or a shovel, or something. The official was ever so polite, and ever so sorry, but the rule was strict, and he could not let us in. It was very embarrassing, for many eyes were on us. But now a richly dressed girl stepped out of the ball-room, inquired into the trouble, and said she could

fix it in a moment. She took Miss Jones to the rob-
ing-room, and soon brought her back in regulation
trim, and then we entered the ballroom with this
benefactress unchallenged.

Being safe, now, I began to puzzle through my
sincere but ungrammatical thanks, when there was
a sudden mutual recognition—the benefactress and
I had met at Allerheiligen. Two weeks had not
altered her good face, and plainly her heart was in
the right place yet, but there was such a difference
between these clothes and the clothes I had seen her
in before, when she was walking thirty miles a day
in the Black Forest, that it was quite natural that I
had failed to recognize her sooner. I had on *my*
other suit, too, but my German would betray me to
a person who had heard it once, anyway. She
brought her brother and sister, and they made our
way smooth for that evening.

Well—months afterward, I was driving through
the streets of Munich in a cab with a German lady,
one day, when she said:

"There, that is Prince Ludwig and his wife, walking along there."

Everybody was bowing to them—cabmen, little
children, and everybody else—and they were returning all the bows and overlooking nobody, when a
young lady met them and made a deep courtesy.

"That is probably one of the ladies of the court,"
said my German friend.

I said:

"She is an honor to it, then. I know her. I
don't know her name, but I know *her*. I have

known her at Allerheiligen and Baden-Baden. She ought to be an Empress, but she may be only a Duchess; it is the way things go in this world."

If one asks a German a civil question, he will be quite sure to get a civil answer. If you stop a German in the street and ask him to direct you to a certain place, he shows no sign of feeling offended. If the place be difficult to find, ten to one the man will drop his own matters and go with you and show you.

In London, too, many a time, strangers have walked several blocks with me to show me my way.

There is something very real about this sort of politeness. Quite often, in Germany, shopkeepers who could not furnish me the article I wanted have sent one of their employees with me to show me a place where it could be had.

CHAPTER XIX

HOWEVER, I wander from the raft. We made the port of Neckarsteinach in good season, and went to the hotel and ordered a trout dinner, the same to be ready against our return from a two-hour pedestrian excursion to the village and castle of Dilsberg, a mile distant, on the other side of the river. I do not mean that we proposed to be two hours making two miles—no, we meant to employ most of the time in inspecting Dilsberg.

For Dilsberg is a quaint place. It is most quaintly and picturesquely situated, too. Imagine the beautiful river before you; then a few rods of brilliant green sward on its opposite shore; then a sudden hill—no preparatory gently rising slopes, but a sort of instantaneous hill—a hill two hundred and fifty or three hundred feet high, as round as a bowl, with the same taper upward that an inverted bowl has, and with about the same relation of height to diameter that distinguishes a bowl of good honest depth—a hill which is thickly clothed with green bushes—a comely, shapely hill, rising abruptly out of the dead level of the surrounding green plains, visible from a great distance down the bends of the river, and with just exactly room on the top of its head for its steepled and turreted and roof-clustered cap of architecture, which same is tightly jammed and compacted within the perfectly round hoop of the ancient village wall.

There is no house outside the wall on the whole hill, or any vestige of a former house; all the houses are inside the wall, but there isn't room for another one. It is really a finished town, and has been finished a very long time. There is no space between the wall and the first circle of buildings; no, the village wall is itself the rear wall of the first circle of buildings, and the roofs jut a little over the wall and thus furnish it with eaves. The general level of the massed roofs is gracefully broken and relieved by the dominating towers of the ruined castle and the tall spires of a couple of churches; so, from a distance Dilsberg has rather more the look of a king's crown than a cap. That lofty green eminence and its quaint coronet form quite a striking picture, you may be sure, in the flush of the evening sun.

We crossed over in a boat and began the ascent by a narrow, steep path which plunged us at once into the leafy deeps of the bushes. But they were not cool deeps by any means, for the sun's rays were weltering hot and there was little or no breeze to temper them. As we panted up the sharp ascent, we met brown, bareheaded and barefooted boys and girls, occasionally, and sometimes men; they came upon us without warning, they gave us good day, flashed out of sight in the bushes, and were gone as suddenly and mysteriously as they had come. They were bound for the other side of the river to work. This path had been traveled by many generations of these people. They have always gone down to the valley to earn their bread, but they have always climbed their hill again to eat it, and to sleep in their snug town.

It is said that the Dilsbergers do not emigrate much; they find that living up there above the world, in their peaceful nest, is pleasanter than living down in the troublous world. The seven hundred inhabitants are all blood-kin to each other, too; they have always been blood-kin to each other for fifteen hundred years; they are simply one large family, and they like the home folks better than they like strangers, hence they persistently stay at home. It has been said that for ages Dilsberg has been merely a thriving and diligent idiot-factory. I saw no idiots there, but the captain said, "Because of late years the government has taken to lugging them off to asylums and otherwheres; and government wants to cripple the factory, too, and is trying to get these Dilsbergers to marry out of the family, but they don't like to."

The captain probably imagined all this, as modern science denies that the intermarrying of relatives deteriorates the stock.

Arrived within the wall, we found the usual village sights and life. We moved along a narrow, crooked lane which had been paved in the Middle Ages. A strapping, ruddy girl was beating flax or some such stuff in a little bit of a goods-box of a barn, and she swung her flail with a will—if it was a flail; I was not farmer enough to know what she was at; a frowsy, barelegged girl was herding half a dozen geese with a stick—driving them along the lane and keeping them out of the dwellings; a cooper was at work in a shop which I know he did not make so large a thing as a hogshead in, for there was not room. In the front rooms of dwellings girls and women were cooking or spinning, and ducks and chickens were waddling in and out, over the threshold, picking up chance crumbs and holding pleasant converse; a very old and wrinkled man sat asleep before his door, with his chin upon his breast and his extinguished pipe in his lap; soiled children were playing in the dirt everywhere along the lane, unmindful of the sun.

Except the sleeping old man, everybody was at work, but the place was very still and peaceful, nevertheless; so still that the distant cackle of the successful hen smote upon the ear but little dulled by intervening sounds. That commonest of village sights was lacking here—the public pump, with its great stone tank or trough of limpid water, and its group of gossiping pitcher-bearers; for there is no well or fountain or spring on this tall hill; cisterns of rain-water are used.

Our alpenstocks and muslin tails compelled attention, and as we moved through the village we gathered a considerable procession of little boys and girls, and so went in some state to the castle. It proved to be an extensive pile of crumbling walls, arches, and towers, massive, properly grouped for picturesque effect, weedy, grass-grown, and satisfactory. The children acted as guides; they walked us along the top of the highest wall, then took us up into a high tower and showed us a wide and beautiful landscape, made up of wavy distances of woody hills, and a nearer prospect of undulating expanses of green lowlands, on the one hand, and castle-graced crags and ridges on the other, with the shining curves of the Neckar flowing between. But the principal show, the chief pride of the children, was the ancient and empty well in the grass-grown court of the castle. Its massive stone curb stands up three or four feet above-ground, and is whole and uninjured. The children said that in the Middle Ages this well was four hundred feet deep, and furnished all the village with an abundant supply of water, in war and peace. They said that in that old day its bottom was below the level of the Neckar, hence the water-supply was inexhaustible.

But there were some who believed it had never been a well at all, and was never deeper than it is now—eighty feet; that at that depth a subterranean passage branched from it and descended gradually to a remote place in the valley, where it opened into somebody's cellar or other hidden recess, and that the secret of this locality is now lost. Those who hold this belief say that herein lies the explanation that Dilsberg, besieged by Tilly and many a soldier before him, was never taken: after the longest and closest sieges the besiegers were astonished to perceive that the besieged were as fat and hearty as ever, and as well furnished with munitions of war—therefore it must be that the Dilsbergers had been bringing these things in through the subterranean passage all the time.

The children said that there was in truth a subterranean outlet down there, and they would prove it. So they set a great truss of straw on fire and threw it down the well, while we leaned on the curb and watched the glowing mass descend. It struck bottom and gradually burned out. No smoke came up. The children clapped their hands and said:

"You see! Nothing makes so much smoke as burning straw—now where did the smoke go to, if there is no subterranean outlet?"

So it seemed quite evident that the subterranean outlet indeed existed. But the· finest thing within the ruin's limits was a noble linden, which the children said was four hundred years old, and no doubt it was. It had a mighty trunk and a mighty spread of limb and foliage. The limbs near the ground were nearly the thickness of a barrel.

That tree had witnessed the assaults of men in mail—how remote such a time seems, and how ungraspable is the fact that real men ever did fight in real armor!—and it had seen the time when these broken arches and crumbling battlements were a trim and strong and stately fortress, fluttering its gay banners in the sun, and peopled with vigorous humanity—how impossibly long ago that seems! —and here it stands yet, and possibly may still be standing here, sunning itself and dreaming its historical dreams, when to-day shall have been joined to the days called "ancient."

Well, we sat down under the tree to smoke, and the captain delivered himself of his legend:

MARK TWAIN

THE LEGEND OF DILSBERG CASTLE

It was to this effect. In the old times there was once a great company assembled at the castle, and festivity ran high. Of course there was a haunted chamber in the castle, and one day the talk fell upon that. It was said that whoever slept in it would not wake again for fifty years. Now when a young knight named Conrad von Geisberg heard this, he said that if the castle were his he would destroy that chamber, so that no foolish person might have the chance to bring so dreadful a misfortune upon himself and afflict such as loved him with the memory of it. Straightway, the company privately laid their heads together to contrive some way to get this superstitious young man to sleep in that chamber.

And they succeeded—in this way. They persuaded his betrothed, a lovely mischievous young creature, niece of the lord of the castle, to help them in their plot. She presently took him aside and had speech with him. She used all her persuasions, but could not shake him; he said his belief was firm, that if he should sleep there he would wake no more for fifty years, and it made him shudder to think of it. Catharina began to weep. This was a better argument; Conrad could not hold out against it. He yielded and said she should have her wish if she would only smile and be happy again. She flung her arms about his neck, and the kisses she gave him showed that her thankfulness and her pleasure were very real. Then she flew to tell the company her success, and the applause she received made her glad and proud she had undertaken her mission, since all alone she had accomplished what the multitude had failed in.

At midnight, that night, after the usual feasting, Conrad was taken to the haunted chamber and left there. He fell asleep, by and by.

When he awoke again and looked about him, his heart stood still with horror! The whole aspect of the chamber was changed. The walls were moldy and hung with ancient cobwebs; the curtains and beddings were rotten; the furniture was rickety and ready to fall to pieces. He sprang out of bed, but his quaking knees sunk under him and he fell to the floor.

"This is the weakness of age," he said.

He rose and sought his clothing. It was clothing no longer. The colors were gone, the garments gave way in many places while he was putting them on. He fled, shuddering, into the corridor, and along it to the great hall. Here he was met by a middle-aged stranger of a kind countenance, who stopped and gazed at him with surprise. Conrad said:

"Good sir, will you send hither the lord Ulrich?"

The stranger looked puzzled a moment, then said: "The lord Ulrich?"

"Yes—if you will be so good."

The stranger called—"Wilhelm!" A young serving-man came, and the stranger said to him:

"Is there a lord Ulrich among the guests?"

"I know none of the name, so please your honor."

Conrad said, hesitatingly:

"I did not mean a guest, but the lord of the castle, sir."

The stranger and the servant exchanged wondering glances. Then the former said:

"I am the lord of the castle."

"Since when, sir?"

"Since the death of my father, the good lord Ulrich, more than forty years ago."

Conrad sank upon a bench and covered his face with his hands while he rocked his body to and fro and moaned. The stranger said in a low voice to the servant:

"I fear me this poor old creature is mad. Call some one."

In a moment several people came, and grouped themselves about, talking in whispers. Conrad looked up and scanned the faces about him wistfully.

Then he shook his head and said, in a grieved voice:

"No, there is none among ye that I know. I am old and alone in the world. They are dead and gone these many years that cared for me. But sure, some of these aged ones I see about me can tell me some little word or two concerning them."

Several bent and tottering men and women came nearer and answered his questions about each former friend as he mentioned the names. This one they said had been dead ten years, that one twenty, another thirty. Each succeeding blow struck heavier and heavier. At last the sufferer said:

"There is one more, but I have not the courage to—O my lost Catharina!"

A TRAMP ABROAD

One of the old dames said:

"Ah, I knew her well, poor soul. A misfortune overtook her lover, and she died of sorrow nearly fifty years ago. She lieth under the linden tree without the court."

Conrad bowed his head and said:

"Ah, why did I ever wake! And so she died of grief for me, poor child. So young, so sweet, so good! She never wittingly did a hurtful thing in all the little summer of her life. Her loving debt shall be repaid—for I will die of grief for her."

His head drooped upon his breast. In a moment there was a wild burst of joyous laughter, a pair of round young arms were flung about Conrad's neck and a sweet voice cried:

"There, Conrad mine, thy kind words kill me— the farce shall go no further! Look up, and laugh with us—'twas all a jest!"

And he did look up, and gazed, in a dazed wonderment—for the disguises were stripped away, and the aged men and women were bright and young and gay again. Catharina's happy tongue ran on:

"'Twas a marvelous jest, and bravely carried out. They gave you a heavy sleeping-draught before you went to bed, and in the night they bore you to a ruined chamber where all had fallen to decay, and placed these rags of clothing by you. And when your sleep was spent and you came forth, two strangers, well instructed in their parts, were here to meet you; and all we, your friends, in our disguises, were close at hand, to see and hear, you may be sure. Ah, 'twas a gallant jest! Come, now, and make thee ready for the pleasures of the day. How real was thy misery for the moment, thou poor lad! Look up and have thy laugh, now!"

He looked up, searched the merry faces about him in a dreamy way, then sighed and said:

"I am aweary, good strangers, I pray you lead me to her grave."

All the smile vanished away, every cheek blanched, Catharina sunk to the ground in a swoon.

All day the people went about the castle with troubled faces, and communed together in undertones. A painful hush pervaded the place which had lately been so full of cheery life. Each in his turn tried to arouse Conrad out of his hallucination and bring him to himself; but all the answer any got was a meek, bewildered stare, and then the words:

"Good stranger, I have no friends, all are at rest these many years; ye speak me fair, ye mean me well, but I know ye not; I am alone and forlorn in the world—prithee lead me to her grave."

During two years Conrad spent his days, from the early morning till the night, under the linden tree, mourning over the imaginary grave of his Catharina. Catharina was the only company of the harmless madman. He was very friendly toward her because, as he said, in some ways she reminded him of his Catharina whom he had lost "fifty years ago." He often said:

"She was so gay, so happy-hearted—but you never smile; and always when you think I am not looking, you cry."

When Conrad died, they buried him under the linden, according to his directions, so that he might rest "near his poor Catharina." Then Catharina sat under the linden alone, every day and all day long, a great many years, speaking to no one, and never smiling; and at last her long repentance was rewarded with death, and she was buried by Conrad's side.

Harris pleased the captain by saying it was a good legend; and pleased him further by adding:

"Now that I have seen this mighty tree, vigorous with its four hundred years, I feel a desire to believe the legend for *its* sake; so I will humor the desire, and consider that the tree really watches over those poor hearts and feels a sort of human tenderness for them."

We returned to Neckarsteinach, plunged our hot heads into the trough at the town pump, and then went to the hotel and ate our trout dinner in leisurely comfort, in the garden, with the beautiful Neckar flowing at our feet, the quaint Dilsberg looming beyond, and the graceful towers and battlements of a couple of medieval castles (called the "Swallow's Nest"[1] and "The Brothers") assisting the rugged scenery of a bend of the river down to our right. We got to sea in season to make the eight-mile run to Heidelberg before the night shut down. We sailed by the hotel in the mellow glow of sunset, and came slashing down with the mad current into the narrow passage between the dikes. I believed I could shoot

[1] The seeker after information is referred to Appendix E for our captain's legend of the "Swallow's Nest" and "The Brothers."

the bridge myself, so I went to the forward triplet of logs and relieved the pilot of his pole and his responsibility.

We went tearing along in a most exhilarating way, and I performed the delicate duties of my office very well indeed for a first attempt; but perceiving, presently, that I really was going to shoot the bridge itself instead of the archway under it, I judiciously stepped ashore. The next moment I had my long-coveted desire: I saw a raft wrecked. It hit the pier in the center and went all to smash and scatteration like a box of matches struck by lightning.

I was the only one of our party who saw this grand sight; the others were attitudinizing, for the benefit of the long rank of young ladies who were promenading on the bank, and so they lost it. But I helped to fish them out of the river, down below the bridge, and then described it to them as well as I could.

They were not interested, though. They said they were wet and felt ridiculous and did not care anything for descriptions of scenery. The young ladies, and other people, crowded around and showed a great deal of sympathy, but that did not help matters; for my friends said they did not want sympathy, they wanted a back alley and solitude.

CHAPTER XX

NEXT morning brought good news—our trunks had arrived from Hamburg at last. Let this be a warning to the reader. The Germans are very conscientious, and this trait makes them very particular. Therefore if you tell a German you want a thing done immediately, he takes you at your word; he thinks you mean what you say; so he does that thing immediately—according to his idea of immediately—which is about a week; that is, it is a week if it refers to the building of a garment, or it is an hour and a half if it refers to the cooking of a trout. Very well; if you tell a German to send your trunk to you by "slow freight," he takes you at your word; he sends it by "slow freight," and you cannot imagine how long you will go on enlarging your admiration of the expressiveness of that phrase in the German tongue, before you get that trunk. The hair on my trunk was soft and thick and youthful, when I got it ready for shipment in Hamburg; it was baldheaded when it reached Heidelberg. However, it was still sound, that was a comfort, it was not battered in the least; the baggagemen seemed to be conscientiously careful, in Germany, of the baggage intrusted to their hands. There was nothing now in the way of our departure, therefore we set about our preparations.

Naturally my chief solicitude was about my collection of Ceramics. Of course I could not take it

with me, that would be inconvenient, and dangerous besides. I took advice, but the best brick-a-brackers were divided as to the wisest course to pursue; some said pack the collection and warehouse it; others said try to get it into the Grand Ducal Museum at Mannheim for safe keeping. So I divided the collection, and followed the advice of both parties. I set aside, for the Museum, those articles which were the most frail and precious.

ETRUSCAN
TEAR-JUG

Among these was my Etruscan tear-jug. I have made a little sketch of it here; that thing creeping up the side is not a bug, it is a hole. I bought this tear-jug of a dealer in antiquities for four hundred and fifty dollars. It is very rare. The man said the Etruscans used to keep tears or something in these things, and that it was

HENRI II. PLATE

very hard to get hold of a broken one, now. I also set aside my Henri II. plate. See sketch from my pencil; it is in the main correct, though I think I have foreshortened one end of it a little too much, perhaps. This is very fine and rare; the shape is exceedingly beautiful and unusual. It has wonderful decorations on it, but I am not able to reproduce them. It cost more than the tear-jug, as the dealer said there was not another plate just like it in the world. He said there was much false Henri II. ware around, but that the genuineness of this piece was unquestionable. He showed me its pedigree, or its history, if you please; it was a document which traced this plate's movements all the way down from its birth—showed who bought it, from whom, and what he paid for it—from the first buyer down to me, whereby I saw that it had gone steadily up from thirty-five cents to seven hundred dollars. He said that the whole Ceramic world would be informed that it was now in my possession and would make a note of it, with the price paid. [Read next page.]

There were Masters in those days, but, alas—it is not so now. Of course the main preciousness of this piece lies in its color; it is that old sensuous, pervading, ramifying, interpolating, transboreal blue which is the despair of modern art. The little sketch which I have made of this gem cannot and does not do it justice, since I have been obliged to leave out the color. But I've got the expression, though.

However, I must not be frittering away the reader's time with these details. I did not intend to go into any detail at all, at first, but it is the failing of the true ceramiker, or the true devotee in any department of brick-a-brackery, that once he gets his tongue or his pen started on his darling theme, he cannot well stop until he drops from exhaustion. He has no more sense of the flight of time than has any other lover when talking of his sweetheart. The very "marks" on the bottom of a piece of rare

Old Blue China.

I also set apart my exquisite specimen of Old Blue China This is considered to be the finest example of Chinese art now in existence; I do not refer to the bastard Chinese art of modern times but that noble & pure & genuine art which flourished under the fostering & appreciative care of the Emperors of the Chung-a Lung-Fung dynasty. -

crockery are able to throw me into a gibbering ecstasy; and I could forsake a drowning relative to help dispute about whether the stopple of a departed Buon Retiro scent-bottle was genuine or spurious.

Many people say that for a male person, bric-a-brac hunting is about as robust a business as making doll-clothes, or decorating Japanese pots with decalcomanie butterflies would be, and these people fling mud at that elegant Englishman, Byng, who wrote a book called *The Bric-a-Brac Hunter*, and make fun of him for chasing around after what they choose to call "his despicable trifles"; and for "gushing" over these trifles; and for exhibiting his "deep infantile delight" in what they call his "tuppenny collection of beggarly trivialities"; and for beginning his book with a picture of himself seated, in a "sappy, self-complacent attitude, in the midst of his poor little ridiculous bric-a-brac junk shop."

It is easy to say these things; it is easy to revile us, easy to despise us; therefore, let these people rail on; they cannot feel as Byng and I feel—it is their loss, not ours. For my part I am content to be a brick-a-bracker and a ceramiker—more, I am proud to be so named. I am proud to know that I lose my reason as immediately in the presence of a rare jug with an illustrious mark on the bottom of it, as if I had just emptied that jug. Very well; I packed and stored a part of my collection, and the rest of it I placed in the care of the Grand Ducal Museum in Mannheim, by permission. My Old

Blue China Cat remains there yet. I presented it to that excellent institution.

I had but one misfortune with my things. An egg which I had kept back from breakfast that morning, was broken in packing. It was a great pity. I had shown it to the best connoisseurs in Heidelberg, and they all said it was an antique. We spent a day or two in farewell visits, and then left for Baden-Baden. We had a pleasant trip of it, for the Rhine valley is always lovely. The only trouble was that the trip was too short. If I remember rightly it only occupied a couple of hours, therefore I judge that the distance was very little, if any, over fifty miles. We quitted the train at Oos, and walked the entire remaining distance to Baden-Baden, with the exception of a lift of less than an hour which we got on a passing wagon, the weather being exhaustingly warm. We came into town on foot.

One of the first persons we encountered, as we walked up the street, was the Rev. Mr. ———, an old friend from America—a lucky encounter, indeed, for his is a most gentle, refined, and sensitive nature, and his company and companionship are a genuine refreshment. We knew he had been in Europe some time, but were not at all expecting to run across him. Both parties burst forth into loving enthusiasms, and Rev. Mr. ——— said:

"I have got a brimful reservoir of talk to pour out on you, and an empty one ready and thirsting to receive what you have got; we will sit up till midnight and have a good satisfying interchange, for

I leave here early in the morning." We agreed to that, of course.

I had been vaguely conscious, for a while, of a person who was walking in the street abreast of us; I had glanced furtively at him once or twice, and noticed that he was a fine, large, vigorous young fellow, with an open, independent countenance, faintly shaded with a pale and even almost imperceptible crop of early down, and that he was clothed from head to heel in cool and enviable snow-white linen. I thought I had also noticed that his head had a sort of listening tilt to it. Now about this time the Rev. Mr. ——— said:

"The sidewalk is hardly wide enough for three, so I will walk behind; but keep the talk going, keep the talk going, there's no time to lose, and you may be sure I will do my share." He ranged himself behind us, and straightway that stately snow-white young fellow closed up to the sidewalk alongside him, fetched him a cordial slap on the shoulder with his broad palm, and sung out with a hearty cheeriness:

"*Americans* for two-and-a-half and the money up! *Hey?*"

The Reverend winced, but said mildly:

"Yes—we are Americans."

"Lord love you, you can just bet that's what *I* am, every time! Put it there!"

He held out his Sahara of a palm, and the Reverend laid his diminutive hand in it, and got so cordial a shake that we heard his glove burst under it.

"Say, didn't I put you up right?"

"Oh, yes."

"Sho! I spotted you for *my* kind the minute I heard your clack. You been over here long?"

"About four months. Have you been over long?"

"*Long?* Well, I should say so! Going on two *years*, by geeminy! Say, are you homesick?"

"No, I can't say that I am. Are you?"

"Oh, *hell*, yes!" This with immense enthusiasm.

The Reverend shrunk a little, in his clothes, and we were aware, rather by instinct than otherwise, that he was throwing out signals of distress to us; but we did not interfere or try to succor him, for we were quite happy.

The young fellow hooked his arm into the Reverend's, now, with the confiding and grateful air of a waif who has been longing for a friend, and a sympathetic ear, and a chance to lisp once more the sweet accents of the mother-tongue—and then he limbered up the muscles of his mouth and turned himself loose—and with such a relish! Some of his words were not Sunday-school words, so I am obliged to put blanks where they occur.

"Yes indeedy! If *I* ain't an American there *ain't* any Americans, that's all. And when I heard you fellows gassing away in the good old American language, I'm ——— if it wasn't all I could do to keep from hugging you! My tongue's all warped with trying to curl it around these ——————— forsaken wind-galled nine-jointed German words here; now I *tell* you it's awful good to lay it over a Christian word once more and kind of let the old

taste soak in. I'm from western New York. My
name is Cholley Adams. I'm a student, you know.
Been here going on two years. I'm learning to be
a horse-doctor! I *like* that part of it, you know,
but ———————— these people, they won't learn a
fellow in his own language, they make him learn in
German; so before I could tackle the horse-doctoring
I had to tackle this miserable language.

"First off, I thought it would certainly give me
the botts, but I don't mind it now. I've got it
where the hair's short, I think; and dontchuknow,
they made me learn Latin, too. Now between you
and me, I wouldn't give a ———————— for all the Latin
that was ever jabbered; and the first thing *I* calcu-
late to do when I get through, is to just sit down
and forget it. 'Twon't take me long, and I don't
mind the time, anyway. And I tell you what! the
difference between school-teaching over yonder and
school-teaching over here—sho! *We* don't know
anything about it! Here you've got to peg and
peg and peg and there just ain't any let-up—and
what you learn here, you've got to *know*, dontchuknow—or else you'll have one of these ——————————
spavined, spectacled, ring-boned, knock-kneed old
professors in your hair. I've been here long *enough*,
and I'm getting blessed tired of it, mind I *tell* you.
The old man wrote me that he was coming over in
June, and said he'd take me home in August,
whether I was done with my education or not, but
durn him, he didn't come; never said why; just
sent me a hamper of Sunday-school books, and
told me to be good, and hold on a while. I don't

take to Sunday-school books, dontchuknow—I don't
hanker after them when I can get pie—but I *read*
them, anyway, because whatever the old man tells
me to do, that's the thing that I'm a-going to *do*,
or tear something, you know. I buckled in and
read all of those books, because he wanted me to;
but that kind of thing don't excite *me*, I like something *hearty*. But I'm awful homesick. I'm homesick from ear-socket to crupper, and from crupper
to hock-joint; but it ain't any use, I've got to stay
here, till the old man drops the rag and gives the
word—yes, *sir*, right here in this ——————
country I've got to linger till the old man says
Come!—and you bet your bottom dollar, Johnny,
it *ain't* just as easy as it is for a cat to have twins!"

At the end of this profane and cordial explosion
he fetched a prodigious "*Whoosh!*" to relieve his
lungs and make recognition of the heat, and then
he straightway dived into his narrative again for
"Johnny's" benefit, beginning, "Well, —————— it
ain't any use talking, some of those old American
words *do* have a kind of a bully swing to them;
a man can *express* himself with 'em—a man can
get at what he wants to *say*, dontchuknow."

When we reached our hotel and it seemed that he
was about to lose the Reverend, he showed so much
sorrow, and begged so hard and so earnestly that
the Reverend's heart was not hard enough to hold
out against the pleadings—so he went away with
the parent-honoring student, like a right Christian,
and took supper with him in his lodgings, and sat in
the surf-beat of his slang and profanity till near

midnight, and then left him—left him pretty well talked out, but grateful "clear down to his frogs," as he expressed it. The Reverend said it had transpired during the interview that "Cholley" Adams's father was an extensive dealer in horses in western New York; this accounted for Cholley's choice of a profession. The Reverend brought away a pretty high opinion of Cholley as a manly young fellow, with stuff in him for a useful citizen; he considered him rather a rough gem, but a gem, nevertheless.

CHAPTER XXI

BADEN-BADEN sits in the lap of the hills, and the natural and artificial beauties of the surroundings are combined effectively and charmingly. The level strip of ground which stretches through and beyond the town is laid out in handsome pleasure grounds, shaded by noble trees and adorned at intervals with lofty and sparkling fountain-jets. Thrice a day a fine band makes music in the public promenade before the Conversation House, and in the afternoon and evening that locality is populous with fashionably dressed people of both sexes, who march back and forth past the great music-stand and look very much bored, though they make a show of feeling otherwise. It seems like a rather aimless and stupid existence. A good many of these people are there for a real purpose, however; they are racked with rheumatism, and they are there to stew it out in the hot baths. These invalids looked melancholy enough, limping about on their canes and crutches, and apparently brooding over all sorts of cheerless things. People say that Germany, with her damp stone houses, is the home of rheumatism. If that is so, Providence must have foreseen that it would be so, and therefore filled the land with these healing baths. Perhaps no other country is so generously supplied with medicinal springs as Germany. Some of these baths are good for one ailment, some for another; and again, peculiar ailments are conquered by combining the individual virtues of several different baths. For instance, for some forms of disease, the patient drinks the native hot water of Baden-Baden, with a spoonful of salt from the Carlsbad springs dissolved in it. That is not a dose to be forgotten right away.

They don't *sell* this hot water; no, you go into the great Trinkhalle, and stand around, first on one foot and then on the other, while two or three young girls sit pottering at some sort of ladylike sewing-work in your neighborhood and can't seem to see you—polite as three-dollar clerks in government offices.

By and by one of these rises painfully, and "stretches"—stretches fists and body heavenward till she raises her heels from the floor, at the same time refreshing herself with a yawn of such comprehensiveness that the bulk of her face disappears behind her upper lip and one is able to see how she is constructed inside—then she slowly closes her cavern, brings down her fists and her heels, comes languidly forward, contemplates you contemptuously, draws you a glass of hot water and sets it down where you can get it by reaching for it. You take it and say:

"How much?"—and she returns you, with elaborate indifference, a beggar's answer:

"Nach Beliebe" (what you please.)

This thing of using the common beggar's trick and the common beggar's shibboleth to put you on your liberality when you were expecting a simple straightforward commercial transaction, adds a little to your prospering sense of irritation. You ignore her reply, and ask again:

"How much?"

—and she calmly, indifferently, repeats:

"*Nach Beliebe.*"

You are getting angry, but you are trying not to show it; you resolve to keep on asking your question till she changes her answer, or at least her annoyingly indifferent manner. Therefore, if your case be like mine, you two fools stand there, and without perceptible emotion of any kind, or any emphasis on any syllable, you look blandly into each other's eyes, and hold the following idiotic conversation:

"How much?"

"*Nach Beliebe.*"

"How much?"

"*Nach Beliebe.*"

"How much?"

"*Nach Beliebe.*"

"How much?"

"*Nach Beliebe.*"

"How much?"

"*Nach Beliebe.*"

"How much?"

"*Nach Beliebe.*"

I do not know what another person would have done, but at this point I gave it up; that cast-iron indifference, that tranquil contemptuousness, conquered me, and I struck my colors. Now I knew she was used to receiving about a penny from manly people who care nothing about the opinions of scullery-maids, and about tuppence from moral cowards; but I laid a silver twenty-five cent piece within her reach and tried to shrivel her up with this sarcastic speech:

"If it isn't enough, will you stoop sufficiently from your official dignity to say so?"

She did not shrivel. Without deigning to look at me at all, she languidly lifted the coin and bit it!—to see if it was good. Then she turned her back and placidly waddled to her former roost again, tossing the money into an open till as she went along. She was victor to the last, you see.

I have enlarged upon the ways of this girl because they are typical; her manners are the manners of a goodly number of the Baden-Baden shopkeepers. The shopkeeper there swindles you if he can, and insults you whether he succeeds in swindling you or not. The keepers of baths also take great and patient pains to insult you. The frowsy woman who sat at the desk in the lobby of the great Friederichsbad and sold bath tickets, not only insulted me twice every day, with rigid fidelity to her great trust, but she took trouble enough to cheat me out of a shilling, one day, to have fairly entitled her to ten. Baden-Baden's splendid gamblers are gone, only her microscopic knaves remain.

An English gentleman who had been living there several years, said:

"If you could disguise your nationality, you would not find any insolence here. These shop-keepers detest the English and despise the Americans; they are rude to both, more especially to ladies of your nationality and mine. If these go shopping without a gentleman or a man-servant, they are tolerably sure to be subjected to petty insolences—insolences of manner and tone, rather than word, though words that are hard to bear are not always wanting. I know of an instance where a shopkeeper tossed a coin back to an American lady with the remark, snappishly uttered, 'We don't take French money here.' And I know of a case where an English lady said to one of these shopkeepers, 'Don't you think you ask too much for this article?' and he replied with the question, 'Do you think you are obliged to buy it?' However, these people are not impolite to Russians or Germans. And as to rank, they worship that, for they have long been used to generals and nobles. If you wish to see to what abysses servility can descend, present yourself before a Baden-Baden shopkeeper in the character of a Russian prince."

It is an inane town, filled with sham, and petty fraud, and snobbery, but the baths are good. I spoke with many people, and they were all agreed in that. I had had twinges of rheumatism unceasingly during three years, but the last one departed after a fortnight's bathing there, and I have never had one since. I fully believe I left my rheumatism in Baden-Baden. Baden-Baden is welcome to it. It was little, but it was all I had to give. I would have preferred to leave something that was catching, but it was not in my power.

There are several hot springs there, and during two thousand years they have poured forth a never-diminishing abundance of the healing water. This water is conducted in pipes to the numerous bath-houses, and is reduced to an endurable temperature by the addition of cold water. The new Friederichs-bad is a very large and beautiful building, and in it one may have any sort of bath that has ever been invented, and with all the additions of herbs and drugs that his ailment may need or that the physician of the establishment may consider a useful thing to put into the water. You go there, enter the great door, get a bow graduated to your style and clothes from the gorgeous portier, and a bath ticket and an insult from the frowsy woman for a quarter; she strikes a bell and a serving-man conducts you down a long hall and shuts you into a commodious room which has a washstand, a mirror, a bootjack, and a sofa in it, and there you undress at your leisure.

The room is divided by a great curtain; you draw this curtain aside, and find a large white marble bathtub, with its rim sunk to the level of the floor, and with three white marble steps leading down into it. This tub is full of water which is as clear as crystal, and is tempered to 28 degrees Réaumur (about 95 degrees Fahrenheit). Sunk into the floor, by the tub, is a covered copper box which contains some warm towels and a sheet. You look fully as white as an angel when you are stretched

out in that limpid bath. You remain in it ten
minutes, the first time, and afterward increase the
duration from day to day, till you reach twenty-
five or thirty minutes. There you stop. The ap-
pointments of the place are so luxurious, the benefit
so marked, the price so moderate, and the insults so
sure, that you very soon find yourself adoring the
Friederichsbad and infesting it.

We had a plain, simple, unpretending, good
hotel, in Baden-Baden—the Hôtel de France—
and alongside my room I had a giggling, cackling,
chattering family who always went to bed just two
hours after me and always got up just two hours
ahead of me. But that is common in German
hotels; the people generally go to bed long after
eleven and get up long before eight. The partitions
convey sound like a drum-head, and everybody
knows it; but no matter, a German family who are
all kindness and consideration in the daytime make
apparently no effort to moderate their noises for
your benefit at night. They will sing, laugh, and
talk loudly, and bang furniture around in the most
pitiless way. If you knock on your wall appeal-
ingly, they will quiet down and discuss the matter
softly among themselves for a moment—then, like
the mice, they fall to persecuting you again, and as
vigorously as before. They keep cruelly late and
early hours, for such noisy folk.

Of course, when one begins to find fault with
foreign people's ways, he is very likely to get a
reminder to look nearer home, before he gets far
with it. I open my note-book to see if I can find

some more information of a valuable nature about Baden-Baden, and the first thing I fall upon is this: "*Baden - Baden* (no date). Lot of vociferous Americans at breakfast this morning. Talking *at* everybody, while pretending to talk among themselves. On their first travels, manifestly. Showing off. The usual signs—airy, easy-going references to grand distances and foreign places. 'Well, *good*-by, old fellow—if I don't run across you in Italy, you hunt me up in London before you sail.'"

The next item which I find in my note-book is this one:

"The fact that a band of 6,000 Indians are now murdering our frontiersmen at their impudent leisure, and that we are only able to send 1,200 soldiers against them, is utilized here to discourage emigration to America. The common people think the Indians are in New Jersey."

This is a new and peculiar argument against keeping our army down to a ridiculous figure in the matter of numbers. It is rather a striking one, too. I have not distorted the truth in saying that the facts in the above item, about the army and the Indians, are made use of to discourage emigration to America. That the common people should be rather foggy in their geography, and foggy as to the location of the Indians, is matter for amusement, maybe, but not of surprise.

There is an interesting old cemetery in Baden-Baden, and we spent several pleasant hours in wandering through it and spelling out the inscriptions on the aged tombstones. Apparently after a **man** has lain there a century or two, and has had a good many people buried on top of him, it is considered that his tombstone is not needed by him any longer. I judge so from the fact that hundreds of old gravestones have been removed from the graves and placed against the inner walls of the cemetery. What artists they had in the old times! They chiseled angels and cherubs and devils and skeletons on the tombstones in the most lavish and generous way—as to supply—but curiously grotesque and outlandish as to form. It is not always easy to tell which of the figures belong among the blest and which of them among the opposite party. But there was an inscription, in French, on one of those old stones, which was quaint and pretty, and was plainly not the work of any other than a poet. It was to this effect:

HERE
REPOSES IN GOD,
CAROLINE DE CLERY,
A RELIGIEUSE OF ST. DENIS,
AGED 83 YEARS—AND BLIND.
THE LIGHT WAS RESTORED TO HER
IN BADEN THE 5TH OF JANUARY,
1839.

We made several excursions on foot to the neighboring villages, over winding and beautiful roads and through enchanting woodland scenery. The woods and roads were similar to those at Heidelberg, but not so bewitching. I suppose that roads and woods which are up to the Heidelberg mark are rare in the world.

Once we wandered clear away to La Favorita Palace, which is several miles from Baden-Baden. The grounds about the palace were fine; the palace was a curiosity. It was built by a Margravine in 1725, and remains as she left it at her death. We wandered through a great many of its rooms, and they all had striking peculiarities of decoration. For instance, the walls of one room were pretty completely covered with small pictures of the Margravine in all conceivable varieties of fanciful costumes, some of them male.

The walls of another room were covered with grotesquely and elaborately figured hand-wrought tapestry. The musty ancient beds remained in the chambers, and their quilts and curtains and canopies were decorated with curious handwork, and the walls and ceilings frescoed with historical and mythological scenes in glaring colors. There was enough crazy and rotten rubbish in the building to make the true brick-a-bracker green with envy. A painting in the dining-hall verged upon the indelicate—but then the Margravine was herself a trifle indelicate.

It is in every way a wildly and picturesquely decorated house, and brimful of interest as a reflection of the character and tastes of that rude bygone time.

In the grounds, a few rods from the palace, stands the Margravine's chapel, just as she left it— a coarse wooden structure, wholly barren of ornament. It is said that the Margravine would give herself up to debauchery and exceedingly fast living

MARK TWAIN

for several months at a time, and then retire to this
miserable wooden den and spend a few months in
repenting and getting ready for another good time.
She was a devoted Catholic, and was perhaps quite
a model sort of a Christian as Christians went then,
in high life.

Tradition says she spent the last two years of her
life in the strange den I have been speaking of, after
having indulged herself in one final, triumphant, and
satisfying spree. She shut herself up there, without
company, and without even a servant, and so ab-
jured and forsook the world. In her little bit of a
kitchen she did her own cooking; she wore a hair
shirt next the skin, and castigated herself with
whips—these aids to grace are exhibited there yet.
She prayed and told her beads, in another little
room, before a waxen Virgin niched in a little box
against the wall; she bedded herself like a slave.

In another small room is an unpainted wooden
table, and behind it sit half-life-size waxen figures of
the Holy Family, made by the very worst artist that
ever lived, perhaps, and clothed in gaudy, flimsy
drapery.[1] The Margravine used to bring her meals
to this table and *dine with the Holy Family*. What
an idea that was! What a grisly spectacle it must
have been! Imagine it: Those rigid, shock-headed
figures, with corpsy complexions and fishy glass
eyes, occupying one side of the table in the con-
strained attitudes and dead fixedness that distinguish
all men that are born of wax, and this wrinkled,

[1] The Saviour was represented as a lad of about fifteen years of
age. This figure had lost one eye.

smoldering old fire-eater occupying the other side, mumbling her prayers and munching her sausages in the ghostly stillness and shadowy indistinctness of a winter twilight. It makes one feel crawly even to think of it.

In this sordid place, and clothed, bedded, and fed like a pauper, this strange princess lived and worshiped during two years, and in it she died. Two or three hundred years ago, this would have made the poor den holy ground; and the church would have set up a miracle-factory there and made plenty of money out of it. The den could be moved into some portions of France and made a good property even now.

CHAPTER XXII

FROM Baden-Baden we made the customary trip into the Black Forest. We were on foot most of the time. One cannot describe those noble woods, nor the feeling with which they inspire him. A feature of the feeling, however, is a deep sense of contentment: another feature of it is a buoyant, boyish gladness; and a third and very conspicuous feature of it is one's sense of the remoteness of the work-day world and his entire emancipation from it and its affairs.

Those woods stretch unbroken over a vast region; and everywhere they are such dense woods, and so still, and so piney and fragrant. The stems of the trees are trim and straight, and in many places all the ground is hidden for miles under a thick cushion of moss of a vivid green color, with not a decayed or ragged spot in its surface, and not a fallen leaf or twig to mar its immaculate tidiness. A rich cathedral gloom pervades the pillared aisles; so the stray flecks of sunlight that strike a trunk here and a bough yonder are strongly accented, and when they strike the moss they fairly seem to burn. But the weirdest effect, and the most enchanting, is that produced by the diffused light of the low afternoon sun; no single ray is able to pierce its way in, then, but the diffused light takes color from moss and foliage, and pervades the place like a faint, green-tinted mist, the theatrical fire of fairyland. The suggestion of mystery and the supernatural which haunts the forest at all times is intensified by this unearthly glow.

We found the Black Forest farmhouses and villages all that the Black Forest stories have pictured them. The first genuine specimen which we came upon was the mansion of a rich farmer and member of the Common Council of the parish or district. He was an important personage in the land and so was his wife also, of course. His daughter was the "catch" of the region, and she may be already entering into immortality as the heroine of one of Auerbach's novels, for all I know. We shall see, for if he puts her in I shall recognize her by her Black Forest clothes, and her burned complexion, her plump figure, her fat hands, her dull expression, her gentle spirit, her generous feet, her bonnetless head, and the plaited tails of hemp-colored hair hanging down her back.

The house was big enough for a hotel; it was a hundred feet long and fifty wide, and ten feet high, from ground to eaves; but from the eaves to the comb of the mighty roof was as much as forty feet, or maybe even more. This roof was of ancient mud-colored straw thatch a foot thick, and was covered all over, except in a few trifling spots, with a thriving and luxurious growth of green vegetation, mainly moss. The mossless spots were places where repairs had been made by the insertion of bright new masses of yellow straw. The eaves projected far down, like sheltering, hospitable wings. Across the gable that fronted the road, and about ten feet above the ground, ran a narrow porch, with a wooden railing; a row of small windows filled with very small panes looked upon the porch. Above were two or three other little windows, one clear up under the sharp apex of the roof. Before the ground-floor door was a huge pile of manure. The door of a second-story room on the side of the house was open, and occupied by the rear elevation of a cow. Was this probably the drawing-room? All of the front half of the house from the ground up seemed to be occupied by the people, the cows, and the chickens, and all the rear half by draught-animals and hay. But the chief feature, all around this house, was the big heaps of manure.

We became very familiar with the fertilizer in the Forest. We fell unconsciously into the habit of judging of a man's station in life by this outward and eloquent sign. Sometimes we said, "Here is a poor devil, this is manifest." When we saw a stately accumulation, we said, "Here is a banker." When we encountered a country-seat surrounded by an Alpine pomp of manure, we said, "Doubtless a duke lives here."

The importance of this feature has not been properly magnified in the Black Forest stories. Manure is evidently the Black-Forester's main treasure—his coin, his jewel, his pride, his Old Master, his ceramics, his bric-a-brac, his darling, his title to public consideration, envy, veneration,

A TRAMP ABROAD

and his first solicitude when he gets ready to make
his will. The true Black Forest novel, if it is ever
written, will be skeletoned somewhat in this way:

SKELETON FOR BLACK FOREST NOVEL

Rich old farmer, named Huss. Has inherited
great wealth of manure, and by diligence has added
to it. It is double-starred in Baedeker.[1] The Black
Forest artist paints it—his masterpiece. The king
comes to see it. Gretchen Huss, daughter and
heiress. Paul Hoch, young neighbor, suitor for
Gretchen's hand—ostensibly; he really wants the
manure. Hoch has a good many cart-loads of the
Black Forest currency himself, and therefore is a
good catch; but he is sordid, mean, and without
sentiment, whereas Gretchen is all sentiment and
poetry. Hans Schmidt, young neighbor, full of
sentiment, full of poetry, loves Gretchen, Gretchen
loves him. But he has no manure. Old Huss forbids him the house. His heart breaks, he goes away
to die in the woods, far from the cruel world—for
he says, bitterly, "What is man, without manure?"

[Interval of six months.]

Paul Hoch comes to old Huss and says, "I am
at last as rich as you required—come and view the
pile." Old Huss views it and says, "It is sufficient
—take her and be happy,"—meaning Gretchen.

[Interval of two weeks.]

Wedding party assembled in old Huss's drawing-
room. Hoch placid and content, Gretchen weeping

---

[1] When Baedeker's guide-books mention a thing and put two stars
(**) after it, it means well worth visiting.　　　　M. T.

I.—13　　　　191

over her hard fate. Enter old Huss's head bookkeeper. Huss says fiercely, "I gave you three
weeks to find out why your books don't balance,
and to prove that you are not a defaulter; the time
is up—find me the missing property or you go to
prison as a thief." Bookkeeper: "I have found it."
"Where?" Bookkeeper (sternly—tragically): "In
the bridegroom's pile!—behold the thief—see him
blench and tremble!" [Sensation.] Paul Hoch:
"Lost, lost!"—falls over the cow in a swoon and is
handcuffed. Gretchen: "Saved!" Falls over the
calf in a swoon of joy, but is caught in the arms of
Hans Schmidt, who springs in at that moment.
Old Huss: "What, you here, varlet? Unhand the
maid and quit the place." Hans (still supporting the
insensible girl): "Never! Cruel old man, know that
I come with claims which even you cannot despise."

Huss: "What, *you?* name them."

Hans: "Then listen. The world had forsaken
me, I forsook the world, I wandered in the solitude
of the forest, longing for death but finding none. I
fed upon roots, and in my bitterness I dug for the
bitterest, loathing the sweeter kind. Digging, three
days agone, I struck a manure mine!—a Golconda,
a limitless Bonanza, of solid manure! I can buy
you *all*, and have mountain ranges of manure left!
Ha-ha, *now* thou smilest a smile!" [Immense sen-
sation.] Exhibition of specimens from the mine.
Old Huss (enthusiastically): "Wake her up, shake
her up, noble young man, she is yours!" Wedding
takes place on the spot; bookkeeper restored to his
office and emoluments; Paul Hoch led off to jail.

The Bonanza king of the Black Forest lives to a good old age, blessed with the love of his wife and of his twenty-seven children, and the still sweeter envy of everybody around.

We took our noon meal of fried trout one day at the Plow Inn, in a very pretty village (Ottenhöfen), and then went into the public room to rest and smoke. There we found nine or ten Black Forest grandees assembled around a table. They were the Common Council of the parish. They had gathered there at eight o'clock that morning to elect a new member, and they had now been drinking beer four hours at the new member's expense. They were men of fifty or sixty years of age, with grave good-natured faces, and were all dressed in the costume made familiar to us by the Black Forest stories; broad, round-topped black felt hats with the brims curled up all round; long red waistcoats with large metal buttons, black alpaca coats with the waists up between the shoulders. There were no speeches, there was but little talk, there were no frivolities; the Council filled themselves gradually, steadily, but surely, with beer, and conducted themselves with sedate decorum, as became men of position, men of influence, men of manure.

We had a hot afternoon tramp up the valley, along the grassy bank of a rushing stream of clear water, past farmhouses, water-mills, and no end of wayside crucifixes and saints and Virgins. These crucifixes, etc., are set up in memory of departed friends, by survivors, and are almost as frequent as telegraph-poles are in other lands.

We followed the carriage-road, and had our usual luck; we traveled under a beating sun, and always saw the shade leave the shady places before we could get to them. In all our wanderings we seldom managed to strike a piece of road at its time for being shady. We had a particularly hot time of it on that particular afternoon, and with no comfort but what we could get out of the fact that the peasants at work away up on the steep mountainsides above our heads were even worse off than we were. By and by it became impossible to endure the intolerable glare and heat any longer; so we struck across the ravine and entered the deep cool twilight of the forest, to hunt for what the guide-book called the "old road."

We found an old road, and it proved eventually to be the right one, though we followed it at the time with the conviction that it was the wrong one. If it was the wrong one there could be no use in hurrying, therefore we did not hurry, but sat down frequently on the soft moss and enjoyed the restful quiet and shade of the forest solitudes. There had been distractions in the carriage-road—school-children, peasants, wagons, troops of pedestrianizing students from all over Germany—but we had the old road to ourselves.

Now and then, while we rested, we watched the laborious ant at his work. I found nothing new in him—certainly nothing to change my opinion of him. It seems to me that in the matter of intellect the ant must be a strangely overrated bird. During many summers, now, I have watched him, when I ought to have been in better business, and I have not yet come across a living ant that seemed to have any more sense than a dead one. I refer to the ordinary ant, of course; I have had no experience of those wonderful Swiss and African ones which vote, keep drilled armies, hold slaves, and dispute about religion. Those particular ants may be all that the naturalist paints them, but I am persuaded that the average ant is a sham. I admit his industry, of course; he is the hardest-working creature in the world—when anybody is looking—but his leather-headedness is the point I make against him. He goes out foraging, he makes a capture, and then what does he do? Go home? No—he goes anywhere but home. He doesn't know where home is. His home may be only three feet away—no matter, he can't find it. He makes his capture, as I have said; it is generally something which can be of no sort of use to himself or anybody else; it is usually seven times bigger than it ought to be; he hunts out the awkwardest place to take hold of it; he lifts it bodily up in the air by main force, and starts, not toward home, but in the opposite direction; not calmly and wisely, but with a frantic haste which is wasteful of his strength; he fetches up against a pebble, and instead of going around it, he climbs over it backward dragging his booty after him, tumbles down on the other side, jumps up in a passion, kicks the dust off his clothes, moistens his hands, grabs his property viciously, yanks it this way, then that, shoves it ahead of him a moment, turns tail and lugs it after him another moment,

gets madder and madder, then presently hoists it
into the air and goes tearing away in an entirely new
direction; comes to a weed; it never occurs to him
to go around it; no, he must climb it; and he does
climb it, dragging his worthless property to the top
—which is as bright a thing to do as it would be for
me to carry a sack of flour from Heidelberg to Paris
by way of Strasburg steeple; when he gets up there
he finds that that is not the place; takes a cursory
glance at the scenery and either climbs down again
or tumbles down, and starts off once more—as
usual, in a new direction. At the end of half an
hour, he fetches up within six inches of the place
he started from and lays his burden down; meantime he has been over all the ground for two yards
around, and climbed all the weeds and pebbles he
came across. Now he wipes the sweat from his
brow, strokes his limbs, and then marches aimlessly
off, in as violent a hurry as ever. He traverses a
good deal of zigzag country, and by and by stum-
bles on his same booty again. He does not remember to have ever seen it before; he looks around to
see which is not the way home, grabs his bundle and
starts; he goes through the same adventures he had
before; finally stops to rest, and a friend comes
along. Evidently the friend remarks that a last
year's grasshopper leg is a very noble acquisition,
and inquires where he got it. Evidently the pro-
prietor does not remember exactly where he did get
it, but thinks he got it "around here somewhere."
Evidently the friend contracts to help him freight it
home. Then, with a judgment peculiarly antic

(pun not intentional), they take hold of opposite ends of that grasshopper leg and begin to tug with all their might in opposite directions. Presently they take a rest and confer together. They decide that something is wrong, they can't make out what. Then they go at it again, just as before. Same result. Mutual recriminations follow. Evidently each accuses the other of being an obstructionist. They warm up, and the dispute ends in a fight. They lock themselves together and chew each other's jaws for a while; then they roll and tumble on the ground till one loses a horn or a leg and has to haul off for repairs. They make up and go to work again in the same old insane way, but the crippled ant is at a disadvantage; tug as he may, the other one drags off the booty and him at the end of it. Instead of giving up, he hangs on, and gets his shins bruised against every obstruction that comes in the way. By and by, when that grasshopper leg has been dragged all over the same old ground once more, it is finally dumped at about the spot where it originally lay, the two perspiring ants inspect it thoughtfully and decide that dried grasshopper legs are a poor sort of property after all, and then each starts off in a different direction to see if he can't find an old nail or something else that is heavy enough to afford entertainment and at the same time valueless enough to make an ant want to own it.

There in the Black Forest, on the mountainside, I saw an ant go through with such a performance as this with a dead spider of fully ten times his own weight. The spider was not quite dead, but too far

gone to resist. He had a round body the size of a
pea. The little ant—observing that I was noticing
—turned him on his back, sunk his fangs into his
throat, lifted him into the air and started vigorously
off with him, stumbling over little pebbles, stepping
on the spider's legs and tripping himself up, dragging him backward, shoving him bodily ahead,
dragging him up stones six inches high instead of
going around them, climbing weeds twenty times his
own height and jumping from their summits—and
finally leaving him in the middle of the road to
be confiscated by any other fool of an ant that
wanted him. I measured the ground which this ass
traversed, and arrived at the conclusion that what
he had accomplished inside of twenty minutes would
constitute some such job as this—relatively speaking—for a man; to wit: to strap two eight-hundred-
pound horses together, carry them eighteen hundred
feet, mainly over (not around) boulders averaging
six feet high, and in the course of the journey
climb up and jump from the top of one precipice
like Niagara, and three steeples, each a hundred
and twenty feet high; and then put the horses
down, in an exposed place, without anybody to
watch them, and go off to indulge in some other
idiotic miracle for vanity's sake.

Science has recently discovered that the ant does
not lay up anything for winter use. This will knock
him out of literature, to some extent. He does not
work, except when people are looking, and only
then when the observer has a green, naturalistic
look, and seems to be taking notes. This amounts

to deception, and will injure him for the Sunday-schools. He has not judgment enough to know what is good to eat from what isn't. This amounts to ignorance, and will impair the world's respect for him. He cannot stroll around a stump and find his way home again. This amounts to idiocy, and once the damaging fact is established, thoughtful people will cease to look up to him, the sentimental will cease to fondle him. His vaunted industry is but a vanity and of no effect, since he never gets home with anything he starts with. This disposes of the last remnant of his reputation and wholly destroys his main usefulness as a moral agent, since it will make the sluggard hesitate to go to him any more. It is strange, beyond comprehension, that so manifest a humbug as the ant has been able to fool so many nations and keep it up so many ages without being found out.

The ant is strong, but we saw another strong thing, where we had not suspected the presence of much muscular power before. A toadstool—that vegetable which springs to full growth in a single night—had torn loose and lifted a matted mass of pine needles and dirt of twice its own bulk into the air, and supported it there, like a column supporting a shed. Ten thousand toadstools, with the right purchase, could lift a man, I suppose. But what good would it do?

All our afternoon's progress had been uphill. About five or half past we reached the summit, and all of a sudden the dense curtain of the forest parted and we looked down into a deep and beautiful gorge and out over a wide panorama of wooded mountains with their summits shining in the sun and their glade-furrowed sides dimmed with purple shade. The gorge under our feet—called Allerheiligen—afforded room in the grassy level at its head for a cozy and delightful human nest, shut away from the world and its botherations, and consequently the monks of the old times had not failed to spy it out; and here were the brown and comely ruins of their church and convent to prove that priests had as fine an instinct seven hundred years ago in ferreting out the choicest nooks and corners in a land as priests have to-day.

A big hotel crowds the ruins a little, now, and drives a brisk trade with summer tourists. We descended into the gorge and had a supper which would have been very satisfactory if the trout had not been boiled. The Germans are pretty sure to boil a trout or anything else if left to their own devices. This is an argument of some value in support of the theory that they were the original colonists of the wild islands off the coast of Scotland. A schooner laden with oranges was wrecked upon one of those islands a few years ago, and the gentle savages rendered the captain such willing assistance that he gave them as many oranges as they wanted. Next day he asked them how they liked them. They shook their heads and said:

"Baked, they were tough; and even boiled, they warn't things for a hungry man to hanker after."

We went down the glen after supper. It is beautiful—a mixture of sylvan loveliness and craggy wildness. A limpid torrent goes whistling down the glen, and toward the foot of it winds through a narrow cleft between lofty precipices and hurls itself over a succession of falls. After one passes the last of these he has a backward glimpse at the falls which is very pleasing—they rise in a seven-stepped stairway of foamy and glittering cascades, and make a picture which is as charming as it is unusual.

CHAPTER XXIII

WE were satisfied that we could walk to Oppenau in one day, now that we were in practice; so we set out next morning after breakfast determined to do it. It was all the way downhill, and we had the loveliest summer weather for it. So we set the pedometer and then stretched away on an easy, regular stride, down through the cloven forest, drawing in the fragrant breath of the morning in deep refreshing draughts, and wishing we might never have anything to do forever but walk to Oppenau and keep on doing it and then doing it over again.

Now, the true charm of pedestrianism does not lie in the walking, or in the scenery, but in the talking. The walking is good to time the movement of the tongue by, and to keep the blood and the brain stirred up and active; the scenery and the woodsy smells are good to bear in upon a man an unconscious and unobtrusive charm and solace to eye and soul and sense; but the supreme pleasure comes from the talk. It is no matter whether one talks wisdom or nonsense, the case is the same, the bulk of the enjoyment lies in the wagging of the gladsome jaw and the flapping of the sympathetic ear.

And what a motley variety of subjects a couple of people will casually rake over in the course of a

day's tramp! There being no constraint, a change
of subject is always in order, and so a body is not
likely to keep pegging at a single topic until it
grows tiresome. We discussed everything we knew,
during the first fifteen or twenty minutes, that
morning, and then branched out into the glad, free,
boundless realm of the things we were not certain
about.

Harris said that if the best writer in the world
once got the slovenly habit of doubling up his
"haves" he could never get rid of it while he
lived. That is to say, if a man gets the habit of
saying "I should have liked to have known more
about it" instead of saying simply and sensibly, "I
should have liked to know more about it," that
man's disease is incurable. Harris said that this
sort of lapse is to be found in every copy of every
newspaper that has ever been printed in English,
and in almost all of our books. He said he had
observed it in Kirkham's grammar and in Ma-
caulay. Harris believed that milk-teeth are com-
moner in men's mouths than those "doubled-up
haves."[1]

That changed the subject to dentistry. I said I
believed the average man dreaded tooth-pulling more
than amputation, and that he would yell quicker
under the former operation than he would under the
latter. The philosopher Harris said that the average

[1] I do not know that there have not been moments in the course of
the present session when I should have been very glad to have
accepted the proposal of my noble friend, and to have exchanged
parts in some of our evenings of work.—[From a Speech of the
English Chancellor of the Exchequer, August, 1879.]

man would not yell in either case if he had an audience. Then he continued:

"When our brigade first went into camp on the Potomac, we used to be brought up standing, occasionally, by an ear-splitting howl of anguish. That meant that a soldier was getting a tooth pulled in a tent. But the surgeons soon changed that; they instituted open-air dentistry. There never was a howl afterward—that is, from the man who was having the tooth pulled. At the daily dental hour there would always be about five hundred soldiers gathered together in the neighborhood of that dental chair waiting to see the performance—and help; and the moment the surgeon took a grip on the candidate's tooth and began to lift, every one of those five hundred rascals would clap his hand to his jaw and begin to hop around on one leg and howl with all the lungs he had! It was enough to raise your hair to hear that variegated and enormous unanimous caterwaul burst out! With so big and so derisive an audience as that, a sufferer wouldn't emit a sound though you pulled his head off. The surgeons said that pretty often a patient was compelled to laugh, in the midst of his pangs, but that they had never caught one crying out, after the open-air exhibition was instituted."

Dental surgeons suggested doctors, doctors suggested death, death suggested skeletons—and so, by a logical process the conversation melted out of one of these subjects and into the next, until the topic of skeletons raised up Nicodemus Dodge out of the deep grave in my memory where he had lain buried and forgotten for twenty-five years. When I was a boy in a printing-office in Missouri, a loose-jointed, long-legged, tow-headed, jeans-clad, countrified cub of about sixteen lounged in one day, and without removing his hands from the depths of his trousers pockets or taking off his faded ruin of a slouch hat, whose broken rim hung limp and ragged about his eyes and ears like a bug-eaten cabbage leaf, stared indifferently around, then leaned his hip against the editor's table, crossed his mighty brogans, aimed at a distant fly from a crevice in his upper teeth, laid him low, and said with composure:

"Whar's the boss?"

"I am the boss," said the editor, following this curious bit of architecture wonderingly along up to its clock-face with his eye.

"Don't want anybody fur to learn the business, 'tain't likely?"

"Well, I don't know. Would you like to learn it?"

"Pap's so po' he cain't run me no mo', so I want to git a show somers if I kin, 'tain't no diffunce what—I'm strong and hearty, and I don't turn my back on no kind of work, hard nur soft."

"Do you think you would like to learn the printing business?"

"Well, I don't re'ly k'yer a durn what I *do* learn, so's I git a chance fur to make my way. I'd jist as soon learn print'n's anything."

"Can you read?"

"Yes—middlin'."

"Write?"

"Well, I've seed people could lay over me thar."

"Cipher?"

"Not good enough to keep store, I don't reckon, but up as fur as twelve-times-twelve I ain't no slouch. 'Tother side of that is what gits me."

"Where is your home?"

"I'm f'm old Shelby."

"What's your father's religious denomination?"

"Him? Oh, he's a blacksmith."

"No, no—I don't mean his trade. What's his *religious* denomination?"

"*Oh*—I didn't understand you befo'. He's a Freemason."

"No, no, you don't get my meaning yet. What I mean is, does he belong to any *church?*"

"*Now* you're talkin'! Couldn't make out what you was a-tryin' to git through yo' head no way. B'long to a *church!* Why, boss, he's ben the pizenest kind of a Free-will Babtis' for forty year. They ain't no pizener ones 'n what *he* is. Mighty good man, pap is. Everybody says that. If they said any diffrunt they wouldn't say it whar *I* wuz—not *much* they wouldn't."

"What is your own religion?"

"Well, boss, you've kind o' got me, thar—and yit you hain't got me so mighty much, nuther. I think 't if a feller he'ps another feller when he's in trouble, and don't cuss, and don't do no mean things, nur noth'n' he ain' no business to do, and don't spell the Saviour's name with a little g, he ain't runnin' no resks—he's about as saift as if he b'longed to a church."

"But suppose he did spell it with a little g—
what then?"

"Well, if he done it a-purpose, I reckon he
wouldn't stand no chance—he *oughtn't* to have no
chance, anyway, I'm most rotten certain 'bout that."

"What is your name?"

"Nicodemus Dodge."

"I think maybe you'll do, Nicodemus. We'll
give you a trial, anyway."

"All right."

"When would you like to begin?"

"Now."

So, within ten minutes after we had first glimpsed
this nondescript he was one of us, and with his coat
off and hard at it.

Beyond that end of our establishment which was
furthest from the street, was a deserted garden,
pathless, and thickly grown with the bloomy and
villainous "jimpson" weed and its common friend
the stately sunflower. In the midst of this mournful
spot was a decayed and aged little "frame" house
with but one room, one window, and no ceiling—it
had been a smoke-house a generation before. Nicodemus was given this lonely and ghostly den as a
bedchamber.

The village smarties recognized a treasure in
Nicodemus, right away—a butt to play jokes on.
It was easy to see that he was inconceivably green
and confiding. George Jones had the glory of per-
petrating the first joke on him; he gave him a cigar
with a firecracker in it and winked to the crowd to
come; the thing exploded presently and swept away

the bulk of Nicodemus's eyebrows and eyelashes. He simply said:

"I consider them kind of seeg'yars dangersome," —and seemed to suspect nothing. The next evening Nicodemus waylaid George and poured a bucket of ice-water over him.

One day, while Nicodemus was in swimming, Tom McElroy "tied" his clothes. Nicodemus made a bonfire of Tom's by way of retaliation.

A third joke was played upon Nicodemus a day or two later—he walked up the middle aisle of the village church, Sunday night, with a staring hand-bill pinned between his shoulders. The joker spent the remainder of the night, after church, in the cellar of a deserted house, and Nicodemus sat on the cellar door till toward breakfast-time to make sure that the prisoner remembered that if any noise was made, some rough treatment would be the consequence. The cellar had two feet of stagnant water in it, and was bottomed with six inches of soft mud.

But I wander from the point. It was the subject of skeletons that brought this boy back to my recollection. Before a very long time had elapsed, the village smarties began to feel an uncomfortable consciousness of not having made a very shining success out of their attempts on the simpleton from "old Shelby." Experimenters grew scarce and chary. Now the young doctor came to the rescue. There was delight and applause when he proposed to scare Nicodemus to death, and explained how he was going to do it. He had a noble new skeleton— the skeleton of the late and only local celebrity,

Jimmy Finn, the village drunkard—a grisly piece of property which he had bought of Jimmy Finn himself, at auction, for fifty dollars, under great competition, when Jimmy lay very sick in the tanyard a fortnight before his death. The fifty dollars had gone promptly for whisky and had considerably hurried up the change of ownership in the skeleton. The doctor would put Jimmy Finn's skeleton in Nicodemus's bed!

This was done—about half past ten in the evening. About Nicodemus's usual bedtime—midnight —the village jokers came creeping stealthily through the jimpson weeds and sunflowers toward the lonely frame den. They reached the window and peeped in. There sat the long-legged pauper, on his bed, in a very short shirt, and nothing more; he was dangling his legs contentedly back and forth, and wheezing the music of "Camptown Races" out of a paper-overlaid comb which he was pressing against his mouth; by him lay a new jewsharp, a new top, a solid india-rubber ball, a handful of painted marbles, five pounds of "store" candy, and a well-gnawed slab of gingerbread as big and as thick as a volume of sheet-music. He had sold the skeleton to a traveling quack for three dollars and was enjoying the result!

Just as we had finished talking about skeletons and were drifting into the subject of fossils, Harris and I heard a shout, and glanced up the steep hillside. We saw men and women standing away up there looking frightened, and there was a bulky object tumbling and floundering down the steep

slope toward us. We got out of the way, and when
the object landed in the road it proved to be a boy.
He had tripped and fallen, and there was nothing
for him to do but trust to luck and take what might
come.

When one starts to roll down a place like that,
there is no stopping till the bottom is reached.
Think of people *farming* on a slant which is so
steep that the best you can say of it—if you want to
be fastidiously accurate—is, that it is a little steeper
than a ladder and not quite so steep as a mansard
roof. But that is what they do. Some of the little
farms on the hillside opposite Heidelberg were stood
up "edgeways." The boy was wonderfully jolted
up, and his head was bleeding, from cuts which it
had got from small stones on the way.

Harris and I gathered him up and set him on a
stone, and by that time the men and women had
scampered down and brought his cap.

Men, women, and children flocked out from
neighboring cottages and joined the crowd; the pale
boy was petted, and stared at, and commiserated,
and water was brought for him to drink and bathe
his bruises in. And such another clatter of tongues!
All who had seen the catastrophe were describing
it at once, and each trying to talk louder than his
neighbor; and one youth of a superior genius ran a
little way up the hill, called attention, tripped, fell,
rolled down among us, and thus triumphantly showed
exactly how the thing had been done.

Harris and I were included in all the descriptions;
how we were coming along; how Hans Gross

shouted; how we looked up startled; how we saw
Peter coming like a cannon-shot; how judiciously we
got out of the way, and let him come; and with
what presence of mind we picked him up and
brushed him off and set him on a rock when the
performance was over. We were as much heroes
as anybody else, except Peter, and were so recognized; we were taken with Peter and the populace
to Peter's mother's cottage, and there we ate bread
and cheese, and drank milk and beer with everybody, and had a most sociable good time; and
when we left we had a hand-shake all around, and
were receiving and shouting back *Leb' wohl's* until a
turn in the road separated us from our cordial and
kindly new friends forever.

We accomplished our undertaking. At half past
eight in the evening we stepped into Oppenau, just
eleven hours and a half out from Allerheiligen—
one hundred and forty-six miles. This is the distance by pedometer; the guide-book and the Imperial Ordnance maps make it only ten and a quarter—a surprising blunder, for these two authorities
are usually singularly accurate in the matter of distances.

CHAPTER XXIV

THAT was a thoroughly satisfactory walk—and the only one we were ever to have which was all the way downhill. We took the train next morning and returned to Baden-Baden through fearful fogs of dust. Every seat was crowded, too; for it was Sunday, and consequently everybody was taking a "pleasure" excursion. Hot! the sky was an oven—and a sound one, too, with no cracks in it to let in any air. An odd time for a pleasure excursion, certainly!

Sunday is the great day on the continent—the free day, the happy day. One can break the Sabbath in a hundred ways without committing any sin.

We do not work on Sunday, because the commandment forbids it; the Germans do not work on Sunday, because the commandment forbids it. We rest on Sunday, because the commandment requires it; the Germans rest on Sunday, because the commandment requires it. But in the definition of the word "rest" lies all the difference. With us, its Sunday meaning is, stay in the house and keep still; with the Germans its Sunday and week-day meanings seem to be the same—rest the *tired part*, and never mind the other parts of the frame; rest the tired part, and use the means best calculated to rest that particular part. Thus: If one's duties have kept him in the house all the week, it will rest him to be out on Sunday; if his duties have required him to read weighty and serious matter all the week, it will rest him to read light matter on Sunday; if his occupation has busied him with death and funerals all the week, it will rest him to go to the theater Sunday night and put in two or three hours laughing at a comedy; if he is tired with digging ditches or felling trees all the week, it will rest him to lie quiet in the house on Sunday; if the hand, the arm, the brain, the tongue, or any other member, is fatigued with inanition, it is not to be rested by adding a day's inanition; but if a member is fatigued with exertion, inanition is the right rest for it. Such is the way in which the Germans seem to define the word "rest"; that is to say, they rest a member by recreating, recuperating, restoring its forces. But our definition is less broad. We all rest alike on Sunday—by secluding ourselves and keeping still, whether that is the surest way to rest the most of us or not. The Germans make the actors, the preachers, etc., work on Sunday. We encourage the preachers, the editors, the printers, etc., to work on Sunday, and imagine that none of the sin of it falls upon us; but I do not know how we are going to get around the fact that if it is wrong for the printer to work at his trade on Sunday it must be equally wrong for the preacher to work at his, since the commandment has made no exception in his favor. We buy Monday morning's paper and read it, and thus encourage Sunday printing. But I shall never do it again.

The Germans remember the Sabbath-day to keep it holy, by abstaining from work, as commanded; we keep it holy by abstaining from work, as commanded, and by also abstaining from play, which is not commanded. Perhaps we constructively *break* the command to rest, because the resting we do is in most cases only a name, and not a fact.

These reasonings have sufficed, in a measure, to mend the rent in my conscience which I made by traveling to Baden-Baden that Sunday. We arrived in time to furbish up and get to the English church before services began. We arrived in considerable style, too, for the landlord had ordered the first carriage that could be found, since there was no time to lose, and our coachman was so splendidly liveried that we were probably mistaken for a brace of stray dukes; else why were we honored with a pew all to ourselves, away up among the very elect at the left of the chancel? That was my first thought. In the pew directly in front of us sat an elderly lady, plainly and cheaply dressed; at her side sat a young lady with a very sweet face, and she also was quite simply dressed; but around us and about us were clothes and jewels which it would do anybody's heart good to worship in.

I thought it was pretty manifest that the elderly lady was embarrassed at finding herself in such a conspicuous place arrayed in such cheap apparel; I began to feel sorry for her and troubled about her. She tried to seem very busy with her prayer-book and her responses, and unconscious that she was out of place, but I said to myself, "She is not succeeding—there is a distressed tremulousness in her voice which betrays increasing embarrassment." Presently the Saviour's name was mentioned, and in her flurry she lost her head completely, and rose and courtesied, instead of making a slight nod as everybody else did. The sympathetic blood surged to my temples and I turned and gave those fine birds what I intended to be a beseeching look, but my feelings got the better of me and changed it into a look which said, "If any of you pets of fortune laugh at this poor soul, you will deserve to be flayed for it." Things went from bad to worse, and I shortly found myself mentally taking the unfriended lady under my protection. My mind was wholly upon her. I forgot all about the sermon. Her embarrassment took stronger and stronger hold upon her; she got to snapping the lid of her smelling-bottle—it made a loud, sharp sound, but in her trouble she snapped and snapped away, unconscious of what she was doing. The last extremity was reached when the collection-plate began its rounds; the moderate people threw in pennies, the nobles and the rich contributed silver, but she laid a twenty-mark gold piece upon the book-rest before her with a sounding slap! I said to myself, "She has parted with all her little hoard to buy the consideration of these unpitying people—it is a sorrowful spectacle." I did not venture to look around this time; but as the service closed, I said to myself, "Let them laugh, it is their opportunity; but at the door of this church they shall see her step into our fine carriage with us, and our gaudy coachman shall drive her home."

Then she rose—and all the congregation stood while she walked down the aisle. She was the Empress of Germany!

No—she had not been so much embarrassed as I had supposed. My imagination had got started on the wrong scent, and that is always hopeless; one is sure, then, to go straight on misinterpreting everything, clear through to the end. The young lady with her imperial Majesty was a maid of honor—and I had been taking her for one of her boarders, all the time.

This is the only time I have ever had an Empress under my personal protection; and considering my inexperience, I wonder I got through with it so well. I should have been a little embarrassed myself if I had known earlier what sort of a contract I had on my hands.

We found that the Empress had been in Baden-Baden several days. It is said that she never attends any but the English form of church service.

I lay abed and read and rested from my journey's fatigues the remainder of that Sunday, but I sent my agent to represent me at the afternoon service, for I never allow anything to interfere with my habit of attending church twice every Sunday.

There was a vast crowd in the public grounds that night to hear the band play the "Fremersberg." This piece tells one of the old legends of the region; how a great noble of the Middle Ages got lost in the mountains, and wandered about with his dogs in a violent storm, until at last the faint tones of a monastery bell, calling the monks to a midnight service, caught his ear, and he followed the direction the sounds came from and was saved. A beautiful air ran through the music, without ceasing, sometimes loud and strong, sometimes so soft that it could hardly be distinguished—but it was always there; it swung grandly along through the shrill whistling of the storm-wind, the rattling patter of the rain, and the boom and crash of the thunder; it wound soft and low through the lesser sounds, the distant ones, such as the throbbing of the convent bell, the melodious winding of the hunter's horn, the distressed bayings of his dogs, and the solemn chanting of the monks; it rose again, with a jubilant ring, and mingled itself with the country songs and dances of the peasants assembled in the convent hall to cheer up the rescued huntsman while he ate his supper. The instruments imitated all these sounds with a marvelous exactness. More than one man started to raise his umbrella when the storm burst forth and the sheets of mimic rain came driving by; it was hardly possible to keep from putting your hand to your hat when the fierce wind began to rage and shriek; and it was *not* possible to refrain from starting when those sudden and charmingly real thunder-crashes were let loose.

I suppose the "Fremersberg" is very low-grade music; I know, indeed, that it *must* be low-grade music, because it so delighted me. warmed me, moved me, stirred me, uplifted me, enraptured me,

that I was full of cry all the time, and mad with
enthusiasm. My soul had never had such a scour-
ing out since I was born. The solemn and majestic
chanting of the monks was not done by instruments,
but by men's voices; and it rose and fell, and rose
again in that rich confusion of warring sounds, and
pulsing bells, and the stately swing of that ever-
present enchanting air, and it seemed to me that
nothing but the very lowest of low-grade music *could*
be so divinely beautiful. The great crowd which
the "Fremersberg" had called out was another evidence that it was low-grade music; for only the
few are educated up to a point where high-grade
music gives pleasure. I have never heard enough
classic music to be able to enjoy it. I dislike the
opera because I want to love it and can't.

I suppose there are two kinds of music—one
kind which one feels, just as an oyster might, and
another sort which requires a higher faculty, a
faculty which must be assisted and developed by
teaching. Yet if base music gives certain of us
wings, why should we want any other? But we do.
We want it because the higher and better like it.
We want it without giving it the necessary time
and trouble; so we climb into that upper tier, that
dress-circle, by a lie; we *pretend* we like it. I know
several of that sort of people—and I propose to be
one of them myself when I get home with my fine
European education.

And then there is painting. What a red rag is to
a bull, Turner's "Slave Ship" was to me, before I
studied art. Mr. Ruskin is educated in art up to a

point where that picture throws him into as mad an
ecstasy of pleasure as it used to throw me into one
of rage, last year, when I was ignorant. His cultivation enables him—and me, now—to see water
in that glaring yellow mud, and natural effects in
those lurid explosions of mixed smoke and flame,
and crimson sunset glories; it reconciles him—and
me, now—to the floating of iron cable-chains and
other unfloatable things; it reconciles us to fishes
swimming around on top of the mud—I mean the
water. The most of the picture is a manifest impossibility—that is to say, a lie; and only rigid
cultivation can enable a man to find truth in a lie.
But it enabled Mr. Ruskin to do it, and it has enabled
me to do it, and I am thankful for it. A Boston newspaper reporter went and took a look at the Slave
Ship floundering about in that fierce conflagration
of reds and yellows, and said it reminded him of a
tortoise-shell cat having a fit in a platter of tomatoes.
In my then uneducated state, that went home to my
non-cultivation, and I thought here is a man with
an unobstructed eye. Mr. Ruskin would have said:
This person is an ass. That is what I would say,
now.[1]

However, our business in Baden-Baden this time,
was to join our courier. I had thought it best to hire
one, as we should be in Italy, by and by, and we

[1] Months after this was written, I happened into the National Gallery in London, and soon became so fascinated with the Turner pictures that I could hardly get away from the place. I went there often,
afterward, meaning to see the rest of the gallery, but the Turner spell
was too strong; it could not be shaken off. However, the Turners
which attracted me most did not remind me of the Slave Ship.

did not know that language. Neither did he. We found him at the hotel, ready to take charge of us. I asked him if he was "all fixed." He said he was. That was very true. He had a trunk, two small satchels, and an umbrella. I was to pay him fifty-five dollars a month and railway fares. On the continent the railway fare on a trunk is about the same it is on a man. Couriers do not have to pay any board and lodging. This seems a great saving to the tourist—at first. It does not occur to the tourist that *somebody* pays that man's board and lodging. It occurs to him by and by, however, in one of his lucid moments.

CHAPTER XXV

NEXT morning we left in the train for Switzerland, and reached Lucerne about ten o'clock at night. The first discovery I made was that the beauty of the lake had not been exaggerated. Within a day or two I made another discovery. This was, that the lauded chamois is not a wild goat; that it is not a horned animal; that it is not shy; that it does not avoid human society; and that there is no peril in hunting it. The chamois is a black or brown creature no bigger than a mustard seed; you do not have to go after it, it comes after you; it arrives in vast herds and skips and scampers all over your body, inside your clothes; thus it is not shy, but extremely sociable; it is not afraid of man, on the contrary, it will attack him; its bite is not dangerous, but neither is it pleasant; its activity has not been overstated—if you try to put your finger on it, it will skip a thousand times its own length at one jump, and no eye is sharp enough to see where it lights. A great deal of romantic nonsense has been written about the Swiss chamois and the perils of hunting it, whereas the truth is that even women and children hunt it, and fearlessly; indeed, everybody hunts it; the hunting is going on all the time, day and night, in bed and out of it. It is poetic foolishness to hunt it with a gun; very few people do that; there is not one man in a million who can hit it with a gun. It is much easier to catch it than it is to shoot it, and only the experienced chamois-hunter can do either. Another common piece of exaggeration is that about the "scarcity" of the chamois. It is the reverse of scarce. Droves of one hundred million chamois are not unusual in the Swiss hotels. Indeed, they are so numerous as to be a great pest. The romancers always dress up the chamois-hunter in a fanciful and picturesque costume, whereas the best way to hunt this game is to do it without any costume at all. The article of commerce called chamois-skin is another fraud; nobody could skin a chamois, it is too small. The creature is a humbug in every way, and everything which has been written about it is sentimental exaggeration. It was no pleasure to me to find the chamois out, for he had been one of my pet illusions; all my life it had been my dream to see him in his native wilds some day, and engage in the adventurous sport of chasing him from cliff to cliff. It is no pleasure to me to expose him, now, and destroy the reader's delight in him and respect for him, but still it must be done, for when an honest writer discovers an imposition it is his simple duty to strip it bare and hurl it down from its place of honor, no matter who suffers by it; any other course would render him unworthy of the public confidence.

Lucerne is a charming place. It begins at the water's edge, with a fringe of hotels, and scrambles up and spreads itself over two or three sharp hills in a crowded, disorderly, but picturesque way, offering to the eye a heaped-up confusion of red roofs, quaint gables, dormer windows, toothpick steeples, with here and there a bit of ancient embattled wall bending itself over the ridges, worm-fashion, and here and there an old square tower of heavy masonry. And also here and there a town clock with only one hand—a hand which stretches straight across the dial and has no joint in it; such a clock helps out the picture, but you cannot tell the time of day by it. Between the curving line of hotels and the lake is a broad avenue with lamps and a double rank of low shade trees. The lake-front is walled with masonry like a pier, and has a railing, to keep people from walking overboard. All day long the vehicles dash along the avenue, and nurses, children, and tourists sit in the shade of the trees, or lean on the railing and watch the schools of fishes darting about in the clear water, or gaze out over the lake at the stately border of snow - hooded mountain peaks. Little pleasure steamers, black with people, are coming and going all the time; and everywhere one sees young girls and young men paddling about in fanciful rowboats, or skimming along by the help of sails when there is any wind. The front rooms of the hotels have little railed balconies, where one may take his private luncheon in calm, cool comfort and look down upon this busy and pretty scene and enjoy it without having to do any of the work connected with it.

Most of the people, both male and female, are in walking costume, and carry alpenstocks. Evidently, it is not considered safe to go about in Switzerland, even in town, without an alpenstock. If the tourist

forgets and comes down to breakfast without his
alpenstock he goes back and gets it, and stands it
up in the corner. When his touring in Switzerland is
finished, he does not throw that broomstick away, but
lugs it home with him, to the far corners of the earth,
although this costs him more trouble and bother than
a baby or a courier could. You see, the alpenstock is
his trophy; his name is burned upon it; and if he has
climbed a hill, or jumped a brook, or traversed a
brickyard with it, he has the names of those places
burned upon it, too. Thus it is his regimental flag,
so to speak, and bears the record of his achieve-
ments. It is worth three francs when he buys it,
but a bonanza could not purchase it after his great
deeds have been inscribed upon it. There are
artisans all about Switzerland whose trade it is to
burn these things upon the alpenstock of the tourist.
And observe, a man is respected in Switzerland
according to his alpenstock. I found I could get no
attention there, while I carried an unbranded one.
However, branding is not expensive, so I soon rem-
edied that. The effect upon the next detachment
of tourists was very marked. I felt repaid for my
trouble.

Half of the summer horde in Switzerland is made
up of English people; the other half is made up of
many nationalities, the Germans leading and the
Americans coming next. The Americans were not
as numerous as I had expected they would be.

The seven-thirty table d'hôte at the great Schweitzerhof furnished a mighty array and variety of nationalities, but it offered a better opportunity to ob-

serve costumes than people, for the multitude sat at immensely long tables, and therefore the faces were mainly seen in perspective; but the breakfasts were served at small round tables, and then if one had the fortune to get a table in the midst of the assemblage he could have as many faces to study as he could desire. We used to try to guess out the nationalities, and generally succeeded tolerably well. Sometimes we tried to guess people's names; but that was a failure; that is a thing which probably requires a good deal of practice. We presently dropped it and gave our efforts to less difficult particulars. One morning I said:

"There is an American party."

Harris said:

"Yes—but name the state.".

I named one state, Harris named another. We agreed upon one thing, however—that the young girl with the party was very beautiful, and very tastefully dressed. But we disagreed as to her age. I said she was eighteen, Harris said she was twenty. The dispute between us waxed warm, and I finally said, with a pretense of being in earnest:

"Well, there is one way to settle the matter—I will go and ask her."

Harris said, sarcastically, "Certainly, that is the thing to do. All you need to do is to use the common formula over here: go and say, 'I'm an American!' Of course she will be glad to see you."

Then he hinted that perhaps there was no great danger of my venturing to speak to her.

I said, "I was only talking—I didn't intend to

approach her, but I see that you do not know what
an intrepid person I am. I am not afraid of any
woman that walks. I will go and speak to this
young girl."

The thing I had in my mind was not difficult. I
meant to address her in the most respectful way and
ask her to pardon me if her strong resemblance to a
former acquaintance of mine was deceiving me; and
when she should reply that the name I mentioned
was not the name she bore, I meant to beg pardon
again, most respectfully, and retire. There would
be no harm done. I walked to her table, bowed to
the gentleman, then turned to her and was about to
begin my little speech when she exclaimed:

"I *knew* I wasn't mistaken—I told John it was
you! John said it probably wasn't, but I knew I
was right. I said you would recognize me presently
and come over; and I'm glad you did, for I shouldn't
have felt much flattered if you had gone out of this
room without recognizing me. Sit down, sit down
—how odd it is—you are the last person I was ever
expecting to see again."

This was a stupefying surprise. It took my wits
clear away, for an instant. However, we shook
hands cordially all around, and I sat down. But
truly this was the tightest place I ever was in. I
seemed to vaguely remember the girl's face, now,
but I had no idea where I had seen it before, or
what name belonged with it. I immediately tried to
get up a diversion about Swiss scenery, to keep her
from launching into topics that might betray that I
did not know her, but it was of no use, she went

WE SHOOK HANDS CORDIALLY.

right along upon matters which interested her more:

"Oh dear, what a night that was, when the sea washed the forward boats away—do you remember it?"

"Oh, *don't* I!" said I—but I didn't. I wished the sea had washed the rudder and the smoke-stack and the captain away—then I could have located this questioner.

"And don't you remember how frightened poor Mary was, and how she cried?"

"Indeed I do!" said I. "Dear me, how it all comes back!"

I fervently wished it *would* come back—but my memory was a blank. The wise way would have been to frankly own up; but I could not bring myself to do that, after the young girl had praised me so for recognizing her; so I went on, deeper and deeper into the mire, hoping for a chance clue but never getting one. The Unrecognizable continued, with vivacity:

"Do you know, George married Mary, after all?"

"Why, no! Did he?"

"Indeed he did. He said he did not believe she was half as much to blame as her father was, and I thought he was right. Didn't you?"

"Of course he was. It was a perfectly plain case. I always said so."

"Why, no you didn't!—at least that summer."

"Oh, no, not that summer. No, you are perfectly right about that. It was the following winter that I said it."

"Well, as it turned out, Mary was not in the least to blame—it was all her father's fault—at least his and old Darley's."

It was necessary to say something—so I said:

"I always regarded Darley as a troublesome old thing."

"So he was, but then they always had a great affection for him, although he had so many eccentricities. You remember that when the weather was the least cold, he would try to come into the house."

I was rather afraid to proceed. Evidently Darley was not a man—he must be some other kind of animal—possibly a dog, maybe an elephant. However, tails are common to all animals, so I ventured to say:

"And what a tail he had!"

"*One!* He had a thousand!"

This was bewildering. I did not quite know what to say, so I only said:

"Yes, he *was* rather well fixed in the matter of tails."

"For a negro, and a crazy one at that, I should say he was," said she.

It was getting pretty sultry for me. I said to myself, "Is it possible she is going to stop there, and wait for me to speak? If she does, the conversation is blocked. A negro with a thousand tails is a topic which a person cannot talk upon fluently and instructively without more or less preparation. As to diving rashly into such a vast subject—"

But here, to my gratitude, she interrupted my thoughts by saying:

"Yes, when it came to tales of his crazy woes, there was simply no end to them if anybody would listen. His own quarters were comfortable enough, but when the weather was cold, the family were sure to have his company—nothing could keep him out of the house. But they always bore it kindly because he had saved Tom's life, years before. You remember Tom?"

"Oh, perfectly. Fine fellow he was, too."

"Yes he was. And what a pretty little thing his child was!"

"You may well say that. I never saw a prettier child."

"I used to delight to pet it and dandle it and play with it."

"So did I."

"You named it. What *was* that name? I can't call it to mind."

It appeared to me that the ice was getting pretty thin, here. I would have given something to know what the child's sex was. However, I had the good luck to think of a name that would fit either sex— so I brought it out:

"I named it Frances."

"From a relative, I suppose? But you named the one that died, too—one that I never saw. What did you call that one?"

I was out of neutral names, but as the child was dead and she had never seen it, I thought I might risk a name for it and trust to luck. Therefore I said:

"I called that one Thomas Henry."

She said, musingly:

MARK TWAIN

"That is very singular . . . very singular."

I sat still and let the cold sweat run down. I was in a good deal of trouble, but I believed I could worry through if she wouldn't ask me to name any more children. I wondered where the lightning was going to strike next. She was still ruminating over that last child's title, but presently she said:

"I have always been sorry you were away at the time—I would have had you name my child."

"*Your* child! Are you married?"

"I have been married thirteen years."

"Christened, you mean."

"No, married. The youth by your side is my son."

"It seems incredible—even impossible. I do not mean any harm by it, but would you mind telling me if you are any over eighteen?—that is to say, will you tell me how old you are?"

"I was just nineteen the day of the storm we were talking about. That was my birthday."

That did not help matters, much, as I did not know the date of the storm. I tried to think of some non-committal thing to say, to keep up my end of the talk, and render my poverty in the matter of reminiscences as little noticeable as possible, but I seemed to be about out of non-committal things. I was about to say, "You haven't changed a bit since then"—but that was risky. I thought of saying, "You have improved ever so much since then"—but that wouldn't answer, of course. I was about to try a shy at the weather, for a saving change, when the girl slipped in ahead of me and said:

230

"How I have enjoyed this talk over those happy old times—haven't you?"

"I never have spent such a half-hour in all my life before!" said I, with emotion; and I could have added, with a near approach to truth, "and I would rather be scalped than spend another one like it." I was holily grateful to be through with the ordeal, and was about to make my good-bys and get out, when the girl said:

"But there is one thing that is ever so puzzling to me."

"Why, what is that?"

"That dead child's name. What did you say it was?"

Here was another balmy place to be in: I had forgotten the child's name; I hadn't imagined it would be needed again. However, I had to pretend to know, anyway, so I said:

"Joseph William."

The youth at my side corrected me, and said: "No, Thomas Henry."

I thanked him—in words—and said, with trepidation:

"O yes—I was thinking of another child that I named—I have named a great many, and I get them confused—this one *was* named Henry Thompson—"

"Thomas Henry," calmly interposed the boy.

I thanked him again—strictly in words—and stammered out:

"Thomas Henry—yes, Thomas Henry was the poor child's name. I named him for Thomas—er—

Thomas Carlyle, the great author, you know—and Henry—er—er—Henry the Eighth. The parents were very grateful to have a child named Thomas Henry."

"That makes it more singular than ever," murmured my beautiful friend.

"Does it? Why?"

"Because when the parents speak of that child now, they always call it Susan Amelia."

That spiked my gun. I could not say anything. I was entirely out of verbal obliquities; to go further would be to lie, and that I would not do; so I simply sat still and suffered—sat mutely and resignedly there, and sizzled—for I was being slowly fried to death in my own blushes. Presently the enemy laughed a happy laugh and said:

"I *have* enjoyed this talk over old times, but you have not. I saw very soon that you were only pretending to know me, and so as I had wasted a compliment on you in the beginning, I made up my mind to punish you. And I have succeeded pretty well. I was glad to see that you knew George and Tom and Darley, for I had never heard of them before and therefore could not be sure that you had; and I was glad to learn the names of those imaginary children, too. One can get quite a fund of information out of you if one goes at it cleverly. Mary and the storm, and the sweeping away of the forward boats, were facts—all the rest was fiction. Mary was my sister; her full name was Mary —— *Now* do you remember me?"

"Yes," I said, "I do remember you now; and

you are as hard-hearted as you were thirteen years
ago in that ship, else you wouldn't have punished
me so. You haven't changed your nature nor your
person, in any way at all; you look just as young
as you did then, you are just as beautiful as you
were then, and you have transmitted a deal of your
comeliness to this fine boy. There—if that speech
moves you any, let's fly the flag of truce, with the
understanding that I am conquered and confess it."

All of which was agreed to and accomplished, on
the spot. When I went back to Harris, I said:

"Now you see what a person with talent and
address can do."

"Excuse me, I see what a person of colossal
ignorance and simplicity can do. The idea of your
going and intruding on a party of strangers, that
way, and talking for half an hour; why I never
heard of a man in his right mind doing such a thing
before. What did you say to them?"

"I never said any harm. I merely asked the girl
what her name was."

"I don't doubt it. Upon my word I don't. I
think you were capable of it. It was stupid in me
to let you go over there and make such an exhibition
of yourself. But you know I couldn't really believe
you would do such an inexcusable thing. What will
those people think of us? But how did you say it?
—I mean the manner of it. I hope you were not
abrupt."

"No, I was careful about that. I said 'My friend
and I would like to know what your name is, if you
don't mind.'"

"No, that was not abrupt. There is a polish about it that does you infinite credit. And I am glad you put me in; that was a delicate attention which I appreciate at its full value. What did she do?"

"She didn't do anything in particular. She told me her name."

"Simply told you her name. Do you mean to say she did not show any surprise?"

"Well, now I come to think, she did show something; maybe it was surprise; I hadn't thought of that—I took it for gratification."

"Oh, undoubtedly you were right; it must have been gratification; it could not be otherwise than gratifying to be assaulted by a stranger with such a question as that. Then what did you do?"

"I offered my hand and the party gave me a shake."

"I saw it! I did not believe my own eyes, at the time. Did the gentlemen say anything about cutting your throat?"

"No, they all seemed glad to see me, as far as I could judge."

"And do you know, I believe they were. I think they said to themselves, 'Doubtless this curiosity has got away from his keeper—let us amuse ourselves with him.' There is no other way of accounting for their facile docility. You sat down. Did they *ask* you to sit down?"

"No, they did not ask me, but I suppose they did not think of it."

"You have an unerring instinct. What else did you do? What did you talk about?"

"Well, I asked the girl how old she was."

"*Un*doubtedly. Your delicacy is beyond praise. Go on, go on—don't mind my apparent misery —I always look so when I am steeped in a profound and reverent joy. Go on—she told you her age?"

"Yes, she told me her age, and all about her mother, and her grandmother, and her other relations, and all about herself."

"Did she volunteer these statistics?"

"No, not exactly that. I asked the questions and she answered them."

"This is divine. Go on—it is not possible that you forgot to inquire into her politics?"

"No, I thought of that. She is a democrat, her husband is a republican, and both of them are Baptists."

"Her husband? Is that child married?"

"She is not a child. She is married, and that is her husband who is there with her."

"Has she any children?"

"Yes—seven and a half."

"That is impossible."

"No, she has them. She told me herself."

"Well, but seven and a *half*? How do you make out the half? Where does the half come in?"

"There is a child which she had by another husband—not this one but another one—so it is a stepchild, and they do not count it full measure."

"Another husband? Has she had another husband?"

"Yes, four. This one is number four."

"I don't believe a word of it. It is impossible, upon its face. Is that boy there her brother?"

"No, that is her son. He is her youngest. He is not as old as he looks; he is only eleven and a half."

"These things are all manifestly impossible. This is a wretched business. It is a plain case: they simply took your measure, and concluded to fill you up. They seem to have succeeded. I am glad I am not in the mess; they may at least be charitable enough to think there ain't a pair of us. Are they going to stay here long?"

"No, they leave before noon."

"There is one man who is deeply grateful for that. How did you find out? You asked, I suppose?"

"No, along at first I inquired into their plans, in a general way, and they said they were going to be here a week, and make trips round about; but toward the end of the interview, when I said you and I would tour around with them with pleasure, and offered to bring you over and introduce you, they hesitated a little, and asked if you were from the same establishment that I was. I said you were, and then they said they had changed their mind and considered it necessary to start at once and visit a sick relative in Siberia."

"Ah, me, you struck the summit! You struck the loftiest altitude of stupidity that human effort has ever reached. You shall have a monument of jackasses' skulls as high as the Strasburg spire if you die before I do. They wanted to know if I was from the same 'establishment' that you hailed from, did they? What did they mean by 'establishment'?"

"I don't know; it never occurred to me to ask."

"Well *I* know. They meant an asylum—an *idiot* asylum, do you understand? So they *do* think there's a pair of us, after all. Now what do you think of yourself?"

"Well, I don't know. I didn't know I was doing any harm; I didn't *mean* to do any harm. They were very nice people, and they seemed to like me."

Harris made some rude remarks and left for his bedroom—to break some furniture, he said. He was a singularly irascible man; any little thing would disturb his temper.

I had been well scorched by the young woman, but no matter, I took it out of Harris. One should always "get even" in some way, else the sore place will go on hurting.

CHAPTER XXVI

THE Hofkirche is celebrated for its organ concerts. All summer long the tourists flock to that church about six o'clock in the evening, and pay their franc, and listen to the noise. They don't stay to hear all of it, but get up and tramp out over the sounding stone floor, meeting late comers who tramp in in a sounding and vigorous way. This tramping back and forth is kept up nearly all the time, and is accented by the continuous slamming of the door, and the coughing and barking and sneezing of the crowd. Meantime, the big organ is booming and crashing and thundering away, doing its best to prove that it is the biggest and loudest organ in Europe, and that a tight little box of a church is the most favorable place to average and appreciate its powers in. It is true, there were some soft and merciful passages occasionally, but the tramp-tramp of the tourists only allowed one to get fitful glimpses of them, so to speak. Then right away the organist would let go another avalanche.

The commerce of Lucerne consists mainly in gimcrackery of the souvenir sort; the shops are packed with Alpine crystals, photographs of scenery, and wooden and ivory carvings. I will not conceal the fact that miniature figures of the Lion of Lucerne are to be had in them. Millions of them. But they are libels upon him, every one of them. There is a subtle something about the majestic pathos of the original which the copyist cannot get. Even the sun fails to get it; both the photographer and the carver give you a dying lion, and that is all. The shape is right, the attitude is right, the proportions are right, but that indescribable something which makes the Lion of Lucerne the most mournful and moving piece of stone in the world, is wanting.

The Lion lies in his lair in the perpendicular face of a low cliff—for he is carved from the living rock of the cliff. His size is colossal, his attitude is noble. His head is bowed, the broken spear is sticking in his shoulder, his protecting paw rests upon the lilies of France. Vines hang down the cliff and wave in the wind, and a clear stream trickles from above and empties into a pond at the base, and in the smooth surface of the pond the lion is mirrored, among the water-lilies.

Around about are green trees and grass. The place is a sheltered, reposeful woodland nook, remote from noise and stir and confusion—and all this is fitting, for lions do die in such places, and not on granite pedestals in public squares fenced with fancy iron railings. The Lion of Lucerne would be impressive anywhere, but nowhere so impressive as where he is.

Martyrdom is the luckiest fate that can befall some people. Louis XVI. did not die in his bed, consequently history is very gentle with him; she is charitable toward his failings, and she finds in him high virtues which are not usually considered to be virtues when they are lodged in kings. She makes him out to be a person with a meek and modest spirit, the heart of a female saint, and a wrong head. None of these qualities are kingly but the last. Taken together they make a character which would have fared harshly at the hands of history if its owner had had the ill luck to miss martyrdom. With the best intentions to do the right thing, he always managed to do the wrong one. Moreover, nothing could get the female saint out of him. He knew, well enough, that in national emergencies he must not consider how he ought to act, as a man, but how he ought to act as a king; so he honestly tried to sink the man and be the king—but it was a failure, he only succeeded in being the female saint. He was not instant in season, but out of season. He could not be persuaded to do a thing while it could do any good—he was iron, he was adamant in his stubbornness then—but as soon as the thing had reached a point where it would be positively harmful to do it, do it he would, and nothing could stop him. He did not do it because it would be harmful, but because he hoped it was not yet too late to achieve by it the good which it would have done if applied earlier. His comprehension was always a train or two behindhand. If a national toe required amputating, he could not see that it needed anything more than poulticing; when others saw that the mortification had reached the knee, he first perceived that the toe needed cutting off—so he cut it off; and he severed the leg at the knee when others saw that the disease had reached the thigh. He was good, and honest, and well meaning, in the matter of chasing national diseases, but he never could overtake one. As a private man, he would have been lovable; but viewed as a king, he was strictly contemptible.

His was a most unroyal career, but the most pitiable spectacle in it was his sentimental treachery to his Swiss guard on that memorable 10th of August, when he allowed those heroes to be massacred in his cause, and forbade them to shed the "sacred French blood" purporting to be flowing in the veins of the red-capped mob of miscreants that was raging around the palace. He meant to be kingly, but he was only the female saint once more. Some of his biographers think that upon this occasion the spirit of Saint Louis had descended upon him. It must have found pretty cramped quarters. If Napoleon the First had stood in the shoes of Louis XVI. that day, instead of being merely a casual and unknown looker-on, there would be no Lion of Lucerne, now, but there would be a well-stocked Communist graveyard in Paris which would answer just as well to remember the 10th of August by.

Martyrdom made a saint of Mary Queen of Scots three hundred years ago, and she has hardly lost all of her saintship yet. Martyrdom made a saint of the trivial and foolish Marie Antoinette, and her biographers still keep her fragrant with the odor of sanctity to this day, while unconsciously proving upon almost every page they write that the only calamitous instinct which her husband lacked, she supplied—the instinct to root out and get rid of an honest, able, and loyal official, wherever she found him. The hideous but beneficent French Revolution would have been deferred, or would have fallen short of completeness, or even might not have happened at all, if Marie Antoinette had made the unwise mistake of not being born. The world owes a great deal to the French Revolution, and consequently to its two chief promoters, Louis the Poor in Spirit and his queen.

We did not buy any wooden images of the Lion, nor any ivory or ebony or marble or chalk or sugar or chocolate ones, or even any photographic slanders of him. The truth is, these copies were so common, so universal, in the shops and everywhere, that they presently became as intolerable to the wearied eye as the latest popular melody usually becomes to the harassed ear. In Lucerne, too, the wood carvings of other sorts, which had been so pleasant to look upon when one saw them occasionally at home, soon began to fatigue us. We grew very tired of seeing wooden quails and chickens picking and strutting around clock-faces, and still more tired of seeing wooden images of the alleged chamois skipping about wooden rocks, or lying upon them in family groups, or peering alertly up from behind them. The first day, I would have bought a hundred and fifty of these clocks if I had had the money—and I did buy three—but on the third day the disease had run its course, I had convalesced, and was in the market once more—trying to sell. However, I had no luck; which was just as well, for the things will be pretty enough, no doubt, when I get them home.

For years my pet aversion had been the cuckoo clock; now here I was, at last, right in the creature's home; so wherever I went that distressing "*hoo*'hoo! *hoo*'hoo! *hoo*'hoo!" was always in my ears. For a nervous man, this was a fine state of things. Some sounds are hatefuler than others, but no sound is quite so inane, and silly, and aggravating as the "*hoo*'hoo" of a cuckoo clock, I think. I bought one, and am carrying it home to a certain person; for I have always said that if the opportunity ever happened, I would do that man an ill turn. What I meant, was, that I would break one of his legs, or something of that sort; but in Lucerne I instantly saw that I could impair his mind. That would be more lasting, and more satisfactory every way. So I bought the cuckoo clock; and if I ever get home with it, he is "my meat," as they say in the mines. I thought of another candidate—a book-reviewer whom I could name if I wanted to—but after thinking it over, I didn't buy him a clock. I couldn't injure his mind.

We visited the two long, covered wooden bridges which span the green and brilliant Reuss just below where it goes plunging and hurrahing out of the lake. These rambling, sway-backed tunnels are very attractive things, with their alcoved outlooks upon the lovely and inspiriting water. They contain two or three hundred queer old pictures, by old Swiss masters—old boss sign-painters, who flourished before the decadence of art.

The lake is alive with fishes, plainly visible to the eye, for the water is very clear. The parapets in front of the hotels were usually fringed with fishers of all ages. One day I thought I would stop and see a fish caught. The result brought back to my mind, very forcibly, a circumstance which I had not thought of before for twelve years. This one:

THE MAN WHO PUT UP AT GADSBY'S

When my odd friend Riley and I were newspaper correspondents in Washington, in the winter of '67, we were coming down Pennsylvania Avenue one night, near midnight, in a driving storm of snow, when the flash of a street-lamp fell upon a man who was eagerly tearing along in the opposite direction. This man instantly stopped and exclaimed:

"This is lucky! You are Mr. Riley, ain't you?"

Riley was the most self-possessed and solemnly deliberate person in the republic. He stopped, looked his man over from head to foot, and finally said:

"I am Mr. Riley. Did you happen to be looking for me?"

"That's just what I was doing," said the man, joyously, "and it's the biggest luck in the world that I've found you. My name is Lykins. I'm one of the teachers of the high school—San Francisco. As soon as I heard the San Francisco postmastership was vacant, I made up my mind to get it—and here I am."

"Yes," said Riley, slowly, "as you have remarked . . . Mr. Lykins . . . here you are. And have you got it?"

"Well, not exactly *got* it, but the next thing to it. I've brought a petition, signed by the Superintendent of Public Instruction, and all the teachers, and by more than two hundred other people. Now I want you, if you'll be so good, to go around with me to the Pacific delegation, for I want to rush this thing through and get along home."

"If the matter is so pressing, you will prefer that we visit the delegation to-night," said Riley, in a voice which had nothing mocking in it—to an unaccustomed ear.

"Oh, to-night, by all means! I haven't got any time to fool around. I want their promise before I go to bed—I ain't the talking kind, I'm the *doing* kind!"

"Yes . . . you've come to the right place for that. When did you arrive?"

"Just an hour ago."

"When are you intending to leave?"

"For New York to-morrow evening—for San Francisco next morning."

"Just so. . . . What are you going to do to-morrow?"

"*Do!* Why, I've got to go to the President with the petition and the delegation, and get the appointment, haven't I?"

"Yes . . . very true . . . that is correct. And then what?"

"Executive session of the Senate at 2 P.M.—got to get the appointment confirmed—I reckon you'll grant that?"

"Yes . . . yes," said Riley, meditatively, "you

are right again. Then you take the train for New York in the evening, and the steamer for San Francisco next morning?"

"That's it—that's the way I map it out!"

Riley considered a while, and then said:

"You couldn't stay . . . a day . . . well, say two days longer?"

"Bless your soul, no! It's not my style. I ain't a man to go fooling around—I'm a man that *does* things, I tell you."

The storm was raging, the thick snow blowing in gusts. Riley stood silent, apparently deep in a reverie, during a minute or more, then he looked up and said:

"Have you ever heard about that man who put up at Gadsby's, once? . . . But I see you haven't."

He backed Mr. Lykins against an iron fence, buttonholed him, fastened him with his eye, like the Ancient Mariner, and proceeded to unfold his narrative as placidly and peacefully as if we were all stretched comfortably in a blossomy summer meadow instead of being persecuted by a wintry midnight tempest:

"I will tell you about that man. It was in Jackson's time. Gadsby's was the principal hotel, then. Well, this man arrived from Tennessee about nine o'clock, one morning, with a black coachman and a splendid four-horse carriage and an elegant dog, which he was evidently fond and proud of; he drove up before Gadsby's, and the clerk and the landlord and everybody rushed out to take charge of him, but he said, 'Never mind,' and jumped out and told the coachman to wait—said he hadn't time to take anything to eat, he only had a little claim against the government to collect, would run across the way, to the Treasury, and fetch the money, and then get right along back to Tennessee, for he was in considerable of a hurry.

"Well, about eleven o'clock that night he came back and ordered a bed and told them to put the horses up—said he would collect the claim in the morning. This was in January, you understand—January, 1834—the 3d of January—Wednesday.

"Well, on the 5th of February, he sold the fine carriage, and bought a cheap second-hand one—said it would answer just as well to take the money home in, and he didn't care for style.

"On the 11th of August he sold a pair of the fine horses—said he'd often thought a pair was better than four, to go over the rough mountain roads with where a body had to be careful about his driving—and there wasn't so much of his claim but he could lug the money home with a pair easy enough.

"On the 13th of December he sold another horse—said two warn't necessary to drag that old light vehicle with—in fact, one could snatch it along faster than was absolutely necessary, now that it was good solid winter weather and the roads in splendid condition.

"On the 17th of February, 1835, he sold the old carriage and bought a cheap second-hand buggy—said a buggy was just the trick to skim along mushy, slushy early spring roads with, and he had always wanted to try a buggy on those mountain roads, anyway.

"On the 1st of August he sold the buggy and bought the remains of an old sulky—said he just wanted to see those green Tennesseans stare and gawk when they saw him come a-ripping along in a sulky—didn't believe they'd ever heard of a sulky in their lives.

"Well, on the 29th of August he sold his colored coachman—said he didn't need a coachman for a sulky—wouldn't be room enough for two in it anyway—and, besides, it wasn't every day that Providence sent a man a fool who was willing to pay nine hundred dollars for such a third-rate negro as that—been wanting to get rid of the creature for years, but didn't like to *throw* him away.

"Eighteen months later—that is to say, on the 15th of February, 1837—he sold the sulky and bought a saddle—said horseback-riding was what the doctor had always recommended *him* to take, and dog'd if he wanted to risk *his* neck going over those mountain roads on wheels in the dead of winter, not if he knew himself.

"On the 9th of April he sold the saddle—said he wasn't going to risk *his* life with any perishable saddle-girth that ever was made, over a rainy, miry April road, while he could ride bareback and know and feel he was safe—always *had* despised to ride on a saddle, anyway.

"On the 24th of April he sold his horse—said 'I'm just fifty-seven to-day, hale and hearty—it would be a *pretty* howdy-do for me to be wasting such a trip as that and such weather as this, on a horse, when there ain't anything in the world so splendid as a tramp on foot through the fresh spring woods and over the cheery mountains, to a man that *is* a man—and I can make my dog carry my claim in a little bundle, anyway, when it's collected. So to-morrow I'll be up bright and early, make my little old collection, and mosey off to Tennessee, on my own hind legs, with a rousing good - by to Gadsby's.'

"On the 22d of June he sold his dog—said 'Dern a dog, anyway, where you're just starting off on a rattling bully pleasure tramp through the summer woods and hills—perfect nuisance—chases the squirrels, barks at everything, goes a-capering and splattering around in the fords—man can't get any chance to reflect and enjoy nature—and I'd a blamed sight ruther carry the claim myself, it's a mighty sight safer; a dog's mighty uncertain in a financial way—always noticed it—well, *good*-by, boys—last call—I'm off for Tennessee with a good leg and a gay heart, early in the morning.'"

There was a pause and a silence—except the noise of the wind and the pelting snow. Mr. Lykins said, impatiently:

"Well?"

Riley said:

"Well—that was thirty years ago."

"Very well, very well—what of it?"

"I'm great friends with that old patriarch. He comes every evening to tell me good - by. I saw him an hour ago—he's off for Tennessee early to-

morrow morning—as usual; said he calculated to
get his claim through and be off before night-owls
like me have turned out of bed. The tears were in
his eyes, he was so glad he was going to see his old
Tennessee and his friends once more."

Another silent pause. The stranger broke it:

"Is that all?"

"That is all."

"Well, for the *time* of night, and the *kind* of
night, it seems to me the story was full long enough.
But what's it all *for?*"

"Oh, nothing in particular."

"Well, where's the point of it?"

"Oh, there isn't any particular point to it. Only,
if you are not in *too* much of a hurry to rush off to
San Francisco with that post-office appointment,
Mr. Lykins, I'd advise you to '*put up at Gadsby's*'
for a spell, and take it easy. Good-by. *God* bless
you!"

So saying, Riley blandly turned on his heel and
left the astonished school-teacher standing there, a
musing and motionless snow image shining in the
broad glow of the street-lamp.

He never got that post-office.

To go back to Lucerne and its fishers, I concluded, after about nine hours' waiting, that the man
who proposes to tarry till he sees somebody hook
one of those well-fed and experienced fishes will find
it wisdom to "put up at Gadsby's" and take it
easy. It is likely that a fish has not been caught on
that lake pier for forty years; but no matter, the
patient fisher watches his cork there all the day

long, just the same, and seems to enjoy it. One may see the fisher-loafers just as thick and contented and happy and patient all along the Seine at Paris, but tradition says that the only thing ever caught there in modern times is a thing they don't fish for at all—the recent dog and the translated cat.

CHAPTER XXVII

CLOSE by the Lion of Lucerne is what they call the "Glacier Garden"—and it is the only one in the world. It is on high ground. Four or five years ago, some workmen who were digging foundations for a house came upon this interesting relic of a long-departed age. Scientific men perceived in it a confirmation of their theories concerning the glacial period; so through their persuasions the little tract of ground was bought and permanently protected against being built upon. The soil was removed, and there lay the rasped and guttered track which the ancient glacier had made as it moved along upon its slow and tedious journey. This track was perforated by huge pot-shaped holes in the bed-rock, formed by the furious washing-around in them of boulders by the turbulent torrent which flows beneath all glaciers. These huge round boulders still remain in the holes; they and the walls of the holes are worn smooth by the long-continued chafing which they gave each other in those old days. It took a mighty force to churn these big lumps of stone around in that vigorous way. The neighboring country had a very different shape, at that time—the valleys have risen up and become hills, since, and the hills have become valleys. The boulders discovered in the pots had traveled a great distance, for there is no rock like them nearer than the distant Rhone Glacier.

For some days we were content to enjoy looking at the blue lake Lucerne and at the piled-up masses of snow-mountains that border it all around—an enticing spectacle, this last, for there is a strange and fascinating beauty and charm about a majestic snow-peak with the sun blazing upon it or the moonlight softly enriching it—but finally we concluded to try a bit of excursioning around on a steamboat, and a dash on foot at the Rigi. Very well, we had a delightful trip to Fluelen, on a breezy, sunny day. Everybody sat on the upper deck, on benches, under an awning; everybody talked, laughed, and exclaimed at the wonderful scenery; in truth, a trip on that lake is almost the perfection of pleasuring. The mountains were a never-ceasing marvel. Sometimes they rose straight up out of the lake, and towered aloft and overshadowed our pygmy steamer with their prodigious bulk in the most impressive way. Not snow-clad mountains, these, yet they climbed high enough toward the sky to meet the clouds and veil their foreheads in them. They were not barren and repulsive, but clothed in green, and restful and pleasant to the eye. And they were so almost straight-up-and-down, sometimes, that one could not imagine a man being able to keep his footing upon such a surface, yet there are paths, and the Swiss people go up and down them every day.

Sometimes one of these monster precipices had

the slight inclination of the huge ship-houses in dockyards—then high aloft, toward the sky, it took a little stronger inclination, like that of a mansard roof—and perched on this dizzy mansard one's eye detected little things like martin boxes, and presently perceived that these were the dwellings of peasants—an airy place for a home, truly. And suppose a peasant should walk in his sleep, or his child should fall out of the front yard?—the friends would have a tedious long journey down out of those cloud-heights before they found the remains. And yet those far-away homes looked ever so seductive, they were so remote from the troubled world, they dozed in such an atmosphere of peace and dreams—surely no one who had learned to live up there would ever want to live on a meaner level.

We swept through the prettiest little curving arms of the lake, among these colossal green walls, enjoying new delights, always, as the stately panorama unfolded itself before us and rerolled and hid itself behind us; and now and then we had the thrilling surprise of bursting suddenly upon a tremendous white mass like the distant and dominating Jungfrau, or some kindred giant, looming head and shoulders above a tumbled waste of lesser Alps.

Once, while I was hungrily taking in one of these surprises, and doing my best to get all I possibly could of it while it should last, I was interrupted by a young and care-free voice:

"You're an American, I think—so'm I."

He was about eighteen, or possibly nineteen; slender and of medium height; open, frank, happy face; a restless but independent eye; a snub nose, which had the air of drawing back with a decent reserve from the silky new-born mustache below it until it should be introduced; a loosely hung jaw, calculated to work easily in the sockets. He wore a low-crowned, narrow-brimmed straw hat, with a broad blue ribbon around it which had a white anchor embroidered on it in front; nobby short-tailed coat, pantaloons, vest, all trim and neat and up with the fashion; red-striped stockings, very low-quarter patent-leather shoes, tied with black ribbon; blue ribbon around his neck, wide-open collar; tiny diamond studs; wrinkleless kids; projecting cuffs, fastened with large oxydized silver sleeve-buttons, bearing the device of a dog's face— English pug. He carried a slim cane, surmounted with an English pug's head with red glass eyes. Under his arm he carried a German grammar— Otto's. His hair was short, straight, and smooth, and presently when he turned his head a moment, I saw that it was nicely parted behind. He took a cigarette out of a dainty box, stuck it into a meer-schaum holder which he carried in a morocco case, and reached for my cigar. While he was lighting, I said:

"Yes—I am an American."

"I knew it—I can always tell them. What ship did you come over in?"

"*Holsatia.*"

"We came in the *Batavia*—Cunard, you know. What kind of a passage did you have?"

"Tolerably rough."

"So did we. Captain said he'd hardly ever seen it rougher. Where are you from?"

"New England."

"So'm I. I'm from New Bloomfield. Anybody with you?"

"Yes—a friend."

"Our whole family's along. It's awful slow, going around alone—don't you think so?"

"Rather slow."

"Ever been over here before?"

"Yes."

"I haven't. My first trip. But we've been all around—Paris and everywhere. I'm to enter Harvard next year. Studying German all the time, now. Can't enter till I know German. I know considerable French—I get along pretty well in Paris, or anywhere where they speak French. What hotel are you stopping at?"

"Schweitzerhof."

"No! is that so? I never see you in the reception-room. I go to the reception-room a good deal of the time, because there's so many Americans there. I make lots of acquaintances. I know an American as soon as I see him—and so I speak to him and make his acquaintance. I like to be always making acquaintances—don't you?"

"Lord, yes!"

"You see it breaks up a trip like this, first rate. I never get bored on a trip like this, if I can make acquaintances and have somebody to talk to. But I think a trip like this would be an awful bore, if a body couldn't find anybody to get acquainted with and talk to on a trip like this. I'm fond of talking, ain't you?"

"Passionately."

"Have you felt bored, on this trip?"

"Not all the time, part of it."

"That's it!—you see you ought to go around and get acquainted, and talk. That's my way. That's the way I always do—I just go 'round, 'round, 'round, and talk, talk, talk—I never get bored. You been up the Rigi yet?"

"No."

"Going?"

"I think so."

"What hotel you going to stop at?"

"I don't know. Is there more than one?"

"Three. You stop at the Schreiber—you'll find it full of Americans. What ship did you say you came over in?"

"*City of Antwerp.*"

"German, I guess. You going to Geneva?"

"Yes."

"What hotel you going to stop at?"

"Hotel de l'Écu de Génève."

"Don't you do it! No Americans there! You stop at one of those big hotels over the bridge—they're packed full of Americans."

"But I want to practise my Arabic."

"Good gracious, do you speak Arabic?"

"Yes—well enough to get along."

"Why, hang it, you won't get along in Geneva—*they* don't speak Arabic, they speak French. What hotel are you stopping at here?"

"Hotel Pension-Beaurivage."

"Sho, you ought to stop at the Schweitzerhof.
Didn't you know the Schweitzerhof was the best
hotel in Switzerland?—look at your Baedeker."

"Yes, I know—but I had an idea there warn't
any Americans there."

"No Americans! Why, bless your soul, it's just
alive with them! I'm in the great reception-room
most all the time. I make lots of acquaintances
there. Not as many as I did at first, because now
only the new ones stop in there—the others go
right along through. Where are you from?"

"Arkansaw."

"Is that so? I'm from New England—New
Bloomfield's my town when I'm at home. I'm
having a mighty good time to-day, ain't you?"

"Divine."

"That's what I call it. I like this knocking
around, loose and easy, and making acquaintances
and talking. I know an American, soon as I see
him; so I go and speak to him and make his acquaintance. I ain't ever bored, on a trip like this, if
I can make new acquaintances and talk. I'm awful
fond of talking when I can get hold of the right kind
of a person, ain't you?"

"I prefer it to any other dissipation."

"That's my notion, too. Now some people like
to take a book and sit down and read, and read, and
read, or moon around yawping at the lake or these
mountains and things, but that ain't my way; no,
sir, if they like it, let 'em do it, I don't object; but as
for me, talking's what *I* like. You been up the Rigi?"

"Yes."

"What hotel did you stop at?"

"Schreiber."

"That's the place!—I stopped there too. *Full* of Americans, *wasn't* it? It always is—always is. That's what they say. Everybody says that. What ship did you come over in?"

"*Ville de Paris*."

"French, I reckon. What kind of a passage did . . . excuse me a minute, there's some Americans I haven't seen before."

And away he went. He went uninjured, too—I had the murderous impulse to harpoon him in the back with my alpenstock, but as I raised the weapon the disposition left me; I found I hadn't the heart to kill him, he was such a joyous, innocent, good-natured numbskull.

Half an hour later I was sitting on a bench inspecting, with strong interest, a noble monolith which we were skimming by—a monolith not shaped by man, but by Nature's free great hand—a massy pyramidal rock eighty feet high, devised by Nature ten million years ago against the day when a man worthy of it should need it for his monument. The time came at last, and now this grand remembrancer bears Schiller's name in huge letters upon its face. Curiously enough, this rock was not degraded or defiled in any way. It is said that two years ago a stranger let himself down from the top of it with ropes and pulleys, and painted all over it, in blue letters bigger than those in Schiller's name, these words:

MARK TWAIN

"Try Sozodont;"
"Buy Sun Stove Polish;"
"Helmbold's Buchu;"
"Try Benzaline for the Blood."

He was captured, and it turned out that he was
an American. Upon his trial the judge said to
him:

"You are from a land where any insolent that
wants to is privileged to profane and insult Nature,
and, through her, Nature's God, if by so doing he
can put a sordid penny in his pocket. But here the
case is different. Because you are a foreigner and
ignorant, I will make your sentence light; if you
were a native I would deal strenuously with you.
Hear and obey:—You will immediately remove every
trace of your offensive work from the Schiller monument; you pay a fine of ten thousand francs; you
will suffer two years' imprisonment at hard labor;
you will then be horsewhipped, tarred and feathered,
deprived of your ears, ridden on a rail to the con-
fines of the canton, and banished forever. The
severest penalties are omitted in your case—not as
a grace to you, but to that great republic which
had the misfortune to give you birth."

The steamer's benches were ranged back to back
across the deck. My back hair was mingling inno-
cently with the back hair of a couple of ladies.
Presently they were addressed by some one and I
overheard this conversation:

"You are Americans, I think? So'm I."

"Yes—we are Americans."

"I knew it—I can always tell them. What ship did you come over in?"

"*City of Chester*."

"Oh, yes—Inman line. We came in the *Batavia*—Cunard, you know. What kind of a passage did you have?"

"Pretty fair."

"That was luck. We had it awful rough. Captain said he'd hardly ever seen it rougher. Where are you from?"

"New Jersey."

"So'm I. No—I didn't mean that; I'm from New England. New Bloomfield's my place. These your children?—belong to both of you?"

"Only to one of us; they are mine; my friend is not married."

"Single, I reckon? So'm I. Are you two ladies traveling alone?"

"No—my husband is with us."

"Our whole family's along. It's awful slow, going around alone—don't you think so?"

"I suppose it must be."

"Hi, there's Mount Pilatus coming in sight again. Named after Pontius Pilate, you know, that shot the apple off of William Tell's head. Guide-book tells all about it, they say. I didn't read it—an American told me. I don't read when I'm knocking around like this, having a good time. Did you ever see the chapel where William Tell used to preach?"

"I did not know he ever preached there."

"Oh, yes, he did. That American told me so. He don't ever shut up his guide-book. He knows

more about this lake than the fishes in it. Besides,
they *call* it 'Tell's Chapel'—you know that yourself. You ever been over here before?"

"Yes."

"I haven't. It's my first trip. But we've been
all around—Paris and everywhere. I'm to enter
Harvard next year. Studying German all the time
now. Can't enter till I know German. This
book's Otto's grammar. It's a mighty good book
to get the *ich habe gehabt haben's* out of. But
I don't really study when I'm knocking around
this way. If the notion takes me, I just run over
my little old *ich habe gehabt, du hast gehabt, er hat
gehabt, wir haben gehabt, ihr haben gehabt, sie haben
gehabt* — kind of 'Now-I-lay-me-down-to-sleep'
fashion, you know, and after that, maybe I don't
buckle to it again for three days. It's awful under-
mining to the intellect, German is; you want to
take it in small doses, or first you know your brains
all run together, and you feel them sloshing around
in your head same as so much drawn butter. But
French is different; *French* ain't anything. I ain't
any more afraid of French than a tramp's afraid of
pie; I can rattle off my little *j'ai, tu as, il a*, and
the rest of it, just as easy as a-b-c. I get along
pretty well in Paris, or anywhere where they speak
French. What hotel are you stopping at?"

"The Schweitzerhof."

"No! is that so? I never see you in the big reception-room. I go in there a good deal of the time,
because there's so many Americans there. I make
lots of acquaintances. You been up the Rigi yet?"

"No."

"Going?"

"We think of it."

"What hotel you going to stop at?"

"I don't know."

"Well, then, you stop at the Schreiber—it's full of Americans. What ship did you come over in?"

"*City of Chester.*"

"Oh, yes, I remember I asked you that before. But I always ask everybody what ship they came over in, and so sometimes I forget and ask again. You going to Geneva?"

"Yes."

"What hotel you going to stop at?"

"We expect to stop in a pension."

"I don't hardly believe you'll like that; there's very few Americans in the pensions. What hotel are you stopping at here?"

"The Schweitzerhof."

"Oh, yes, I asked you that before, too. But I always ask everybody what hotel they're stopping at, and so I've got my head all mixed up with hotels. But it makes talk, and I love to talk. It refreshes me up so—don't it you—on a trip like this?"

"Yes—sometimes."

"Well, it does me, too. As long as I'm talking I never feel bored—ain't that the way with you?"

"Yes—generally. But there are exceptions to the rule."

"Oh, of course. *I* don't care to talk to everybody, *myself*. If a person starts in to jabber-jabber-

jabber about scenery, and history, and pictures, and all sorts of tiresome things, I get the fan-tods mighty soon. I say 'Well, I must be going now—hope I'll see you again'—and then I take a walk. Where you from?"

"New Jersey."

"Why, bother it all, I asked you *that* before, too. Have you seen the Lion of Lucerne?"

"Not yet."

"Nor I, either. But the man who told me about Mount Pilatus says it's one of the things to see. It's twenty-eight feet long. It don't seem reasonable, but he said so, anyway. He saw it yesterday; said it was dying, then, so I reckon it's dead by this time. But that ain't any matter, of course they'll stuff it. Did you say the children are yours—or *hers?*"

"Mine."

"Oh, so you did. Are you going up the . . . no, I asked you that. What ship . . . no, I asked you that, too. What hotel are you . . . no, you told me that. Let me see . . . um. . . . Oh, what kind of a voy . . . no, we've been over that ground, too. Um . . . um . . . well, I believe that is all. *Bonjour*—I am very glad to have made your acquaintance, ladies. *Guten Tag.*"

CHAPTER XXVIII

THE Rigi-Kulm is an imposing Alpine mass, six thousand feet high, which stands by itself, and commands a mighty prospect of blue lakes, green valleys, and snowy mountains—a compact and magnificent picture three hundred miles in circumference. The ascent is made by rail, or horseback, or on foot, as one may prefer. I and my agent panoplied ourselves in walking-costume, one bright morning, and started down the lake on the steamboat; we got ashore at the village of Wäggis, three-quarters of an hour distant from Lucerne. This village is at the foot of the mountain.

We were soon tramping leisurely up the leafy mule-path, and then the talk began to flow, as usual. It was twelve o'clock noon, and a breezy, cloudless day; the ascent was gradual, and the glimpses, from under the curtaining boughs, of blue water, and tiny sailboats, and beetling cliffs, were as charming as glimpses of dreamland. All the circumstances were perfect—and the anticipations, too, for we should soon be enjoying, for the first time, that wonderful spectacle, an Alpine sunrise—the object of our journey. There was (apparently) no real need to hurry, for the guide-book made the walking-distance from Wäggis to the summit only three hours and a

MARK TWAIN

quarter. I say "apparently," because the guide-book had already fooled us once—about the distance from Allerheiligen to Oppenau—and for aught I knew it might be getting ready to fool us again. We were only certain as to the altitudes—we calculated to find out for ourselves how many hours it is from the bottom to the top. The summit is six thousand feet above the sea, but only forty-five hundred feet above the lake. When we had walked half an hour, we were fairly into the swing and humor of the undertaking, so we cleared for action; that is to say, we got a boy whom we met to carry our alpenstocks and satchels and overcoats and things for us; that left us free for business. I suppose we must have stopped oftener to stretch out on the grass in the shade and take a bit of a smoke than this boy was used to, for presently he asked if it had been our idea to hire him by the job, or by the year? We told him he could move along if he was in a hurry. He said he wasn't in such a very particular hurry, but he wanted to get to the top while he was young. We told him to clear out, then, and leave the things at the upper-most hotel and say we should be along presently. He said he would secure us a hotel if he could, but if they were all full he would ask them to build another one and hurry up and get the paint and plaster dry against we arrived. Still gently chaffing us, he pushed ahead, up the trail, and soon disappeared. By six o'clock we were pretty high up in the air, and the view of lake and mountains had greatly grown in breadth and interest. We halted awhile at a little public house, where we had bread and cheese and a quart or two of fresh milk, out on the porch, with the big panorama all before us—and then moved on again.

Ten minutes afterward we met a hot, red-faced man plunging down the mountain, with mighty strides, swinging his alpenstock ahead of him, and taking a grip on the ground with its iron point to support these big strides. He stopped, fanned himself with his hat, swabbed the perspiration from his face and neck with a red handkerchief, panted a moment or two, and asked how far it was to Wäggis. I said three hours. He looked surprised, and said:

"Why, it seems as if I could toss a biscuit into the lake from here, it's so close by. Is that an inn, there?"

I said it was.

"Well," said he, "I can't stand another three hours, I've had enough for to-day; I'll take a bed there."

I asked:

"Are we nearly to the top?"

"Nearly to the *top!* Why, bless your soul, you haven't really started, yet."

I said we would put up at the inn, too. So we turned back and ordered a hot supper, and had quite a jolly evening of it with this Englishman.

The German landlady gave us neat rooms and nice beds, and when I and my agent turned in, it was with the resolution to be up early and make the utmost of our first Alpine sunrise. But of course we were dead tired, and slept like policemen; so when we awoke in the morning and ran to the window it was already too late, because it was half past eleven. It was a sharp disappointment. However, we ordered breakfast and told the landlady to call the Englishman, but she said he was already up and off at daybreak—and swearing mad about something or other. We could not find out what the matter was. He had asked the landlady the altitude of her place above the level of the lake, and she had told him fourteen hundred and ninety-five feet. That was all that was said; then he lost his temper. He said that between —— fools and guide-books, a man could acquire ignorance enough in twenty-four hours in a country like this to last him a year. Harris believed our boy had been loading him up with misinformation; and this was probably the case, for his epithet described that boy to a dot.

We got under way about the turn of noon, and pulled out for the summit again, with a fresh and vigorous step. When we had gone about two hundred yards, and stopped to rest, I glanced to the left while I was lighting my pipe, and in the distance detected a long worm of black smoke crawling lazily up the steep mountain. Of course that was the locomotive. We propped ourselves on our elbows at once, to gaze, for we had never seen a mountain railway yet. Presently we could make out the train. It seemed incredible that that thing should creep straight up a sharp slant like the roof of a house —but there it was, and it was doing that very miracle.

In the course of a couple of hours we reached a

fine breezy altitude where the little shepherd huts had big stones all over their roofs to hold them down to the earth when the great storms rage. The country was wild and rocky about here, but there were plenty of trees, plenty of moss, and grass.

Away off on the opposite shore of the lake we could see some villages, and now for the first time we could observe the real difference between their proportions and those of the giant mountains at whose feet they slept. When one is in one of those villages it seems spacious, and its houses seem high and not out of proportion to the mountain that overhangs them—but from our altitude, what a change! The mountains were bigger and grander than ever, as they stood there thinking their solemn thoughts with their heads in the drifting clouds, but the villages at their feet—when the painstaking eye could trace them up and find them—were so reduced, so almost invisible, and lay so flat against the ground, that the exactest simile I can devise is to compare them to ant-deposits of granulated dirt over-shadowed by the huge bulk of a cathedral. The steamboats skimming along under the stupendous precipices were diminished by distance to the daintiest little toys, the sailboats and rowboats to shallops proper for fairies that keep house in the cups of lilies and ride to court on the backs of bumblebees.

Presently we came upon half a dozen sheep nibbling grass in the spray of a stream of clear water that sprang from a rock wall a hundred feet high, and all at once our ears were startled with a melodious "Lul . . . l . . . l . . . lul-lul-*la*hee-o-o-o!" peal-

ing joyously from a near but invisible source, and
recognized that we were hearing for the first time the
famous Alpine *jodel* in its own native wilds. And
we recognized, also, that it was that sort of quaint
commingling of barytone and falsetto which at home
we call "Tyrolese warbling."

The jodeling (pronounced yodling—emphasis on
the o) continued, and was very pleasant and inspiriting to hear. Now the jodeler appeared—a
shepherd boy of sixteen—and in our gladness and
gratitude we gave him a franc to jodel some more.
So he jodeled and we listened. We moved on, presently, and he generously jodeled us out of sight.
After about fifteen minutes we came across another
shepherd boy who was jodeling, and gave him half
a france to keep it up. He also jodeled us out of
sight. After that, we found a jodeler every ten
minutes; we gave the first one eight cents, the second
one six cents, the third one four, the fourth one a
penny, contributed nothing to Nos. 5, 6, and 7, and
during the remainder of the day hired the rest of
the jodelers, at a franc apiece, not to jodel any more.
There is somewhat too much of this jodeling in the
Alps.

About the middle of the afternoon we passed
through a prodigious natural gateway called the
Felsenthor, formed by two enormous upright rocks,
with a third lying across the top. There was a very
attractive little hotel close by, but our energies were
not conquered yet, so we went on.

Three hours afterward we came to the railway-
track. It was planted straight up the mountain

with the slant of a ladder that leans against a house, and it seemed to us that a man would need good nerves who proposed to travel up it or down it either.

During the latter part of the afternoon we cooled our roasting interiors with ice-cold water from clear streams, the only really satisfying water we had tasted since we left home, for at the hotels on the continent they merely give you a tumbler of ice to soak your water in, and that only modifies its hotness, doesn't make it cold. Water can only be made cold enough for summer comfort by being prepared in a refrigerator or a closed ice-pitcher. Europeans say ice-water impairs digestion. How do they know? —they never drink any.

At ten minutes past six we reached the Kaltbad station, where there is a spacious hotel with great verandas which command a majestic expanse of lake and mountain scenery. We were pretty well fagged out, now, but as we did not wish to miss the Alpine sunrise, we got through with our dinner as quickly as possible and hurried off to bed. It was unspeakably comfortable to stretch our weary limbs between the cool, damp sheets. And how we did sleep!— for there is no opiate like Alpine pedestrianism.

In the morning we both awoke and leaped out of bed at the same instant and ran and stripped aside the window-curtains; but we suffered a bitter disappointment again: it was already half past three in the afternoon.

We dressed sullenly and in ill spirits, each accusing the other of oversleeping. Harris said if we had brought the courier along, as we ought to have done, we should not have missed these sunrises. I said he knew very well that one of us would have had to sit up and wake the courier; and I added that we were having trouble enough to take care of ourselves, on this climb, without having to take care of a courier besides.

During breakfast our spirits came up a little, since we found by the guide-book that in the hotels on the summit the tourist is not left to trust to luck for his sunrise, but is roused betimes by a man who goes through the halls with a great Alpine horn, blowing blasts that would raise the dead. And there was another consoling thing: the guide-book said that up there on the summit the guests did not wait to dress much, but seized a red bed blanket and sailed out arrayed like an Indian. This was good; this would be romantic; two hundred and fifty people grouped on the windy summit, with their hair flying and their red blankets flapping, in the solemn presence of the snowy ranges and the messenger splendors of the coming sun, would be a striking and memorable spectacle. So it was good luck, not ill luck, that we had missed those other sunrises.

We were informed by the guide-book that we were now 3,228 feet above the level of the lake—therefore full two-thirds of our journey had been accomplished. We got away at a quarter past four, P.M.; a hundred yards above the hotel the railway divided; one track went straight up the steep hill, the other one turned square off to the right, with a very slight grade. We took the latter, and followed it more than a mile, turned a rocky corner, and came in sight of a handsome new hotel. If we had gone on, we should have arrived at the summit, but Harris preferred to ask a lot of questions—as usual, of a man who didn't know anything—and he told us to go back and follow the other route. We did so. We could ill afford this loss of time.

We climbed, and climbed; and we kept on climbing; we reached about forty summits, but there was always another one just ahead. It came on to rain, and it rained in dead earnest. We were soaked through and it was bitter cold. Next a smoky fog of clouds covered the whole region densely, and we took to the railway-ties to keep from getting lost. Sometimes we slopped along in a narrow path on the left-hand side of the track, but by and by when the fog blew aside a little and we saw that we were treading the rampart of a precipice and that our left elbows were projecting over a perfectly boundless and bottomless vacancy, we gasped, and jumped for the ties again.

The night shut down, dark and drizzly and cold. About eight in the evening the fog lifted and showed us a well-worn path which led up a very steep rise to the left. We took it, and as soon as we had got far enough from the railway to render the finding it again an impossibility, the fog shut down on us once more.

We were in a bleak, unsheltered place, now, and had to trudge right along, in order to keep warm, though we rather expected to go over a precipice, sooner or later. About nine o'clock we made an important discovery—that we were not in any path.

We groped around a while on our hands and knees, but could not find it; so we sat down in the mud and the wet scant grass to wait.

We were terrified into this by being suddenly confronted with a vast body which showed itself vaguely for an instant and in the next instant was smothered in the fog again. It was really the hotel we were after, monstrously magnified by the fog, but we took it for the face of a precipice, and decided not to try to claw up it.

We sat there an hour, with chattering teeth and quivering bodies, and quarreled over all sorts of trifles, but gave most of our attention to abusing each other for the stupidity of deserting the railway-track. We sat with our backs to that precipice, because what little wind there was came from that quarter. At some time or other the fog thinned a little; we did not know when, for we were facing the empty universe and the thinness could not show; but at last Harris happened to look around, and there stood a huge, dim, spectral hotel where the precipice had been. One could faintly discern the windows and chimneys, and a dull blur of lights. Our first emotion was deep, unutterable gratitude, our next was a foolish rage, born of the suspicion that possibly the hotel had been visible three-quarters of an hour while we sat there in those cold puddles quarreling.

Yes, it was the Rigi-Kulm hotel—the one that occupies the extreme summit, and whose remote little sparkle of lights we had often seen glinting high aloft among the stars from our balcony away down yonder in Lucerne. The crusty portier and the crusty clerks gave us the surly reception which their kind deal in in prosperous times, but by mollifying them with an extra display of obsequiousness and servility we finally got them to show us to the room which our boy had engaged for us.

We got into some dry clothing, and while our supper was preparing we loafed forsakenly through a couple of vast cavernous drawing-rooms, one of which had a stove in it. This stove was in a corner, and densely walled around with people. We could not get near the fire, so we moved at large in the arctic spaces, among a multitude of people who sat silent, smileless, forlorn, and shivering—thinking what fools they were to come, perhaps. There were some Americans and some Germans, but one could see that the great majority were English.

We lounged into an apartment where there was a great crowd, to see what was going on. It was a memento-magazine. The tourists were eagerly buying all sorts and styles of paper-cutters, marked "Souvenir of the Rigi," with handles made of the little curved horn of the ostensible chamois; there were all manner of wooden goblets and such things, similarly marked. I was going to buy a paper-cutter, but I believed I could remember the cold comfort of the Rigi-Kulm without it, so I smothered the impulse.

Supper warmed us, and we went immediately to bed—but first, as Mr. Baedeker requests all tourists to call his attention to any errors which they may find in his guide-books, I dropped him a line to inform him that when he said the foot journey from

Wäggis to the summit was only three hours and a quarter, he missed it by just about three days. I had previously informed him of his mistake about the distance from Allerheiligen to Oppenau, and had also informed the Ordnance Department of the German government of the same error in the imperial maps. I will add, here, that I never got any answer to these letters, or any thanks from either of those sources; and, what is still more discourteous, these corrections have not been made, either in the maps or the guide-books. But I will write again when I get time, for my letters may have miscarried.

We curled up in the clammy beds, and went to sleep without rocking. We were so sodden with fatigue that we never stirred nor turned over till the blooming blasts of the Alpine horn aroused us. It may well be imagined that we did not lose any time. We snatched on a few odds and ends of clothing, cocooned ourselves in the proper red blankets, and plunged along the halls and out into the whistling wind bareheaded. We saw a tall wooden scaffolding on the very peak of the summit, a hundred yards away, and made for it. We rushed up the stairs to the top of this scaffolding, and stood there, above the vast outlying world, with hair flying and ruddy blankets waving and cracking in the fierce breeze.

"Fifteen minutes too late, at last!" said Harris, in a vexed voice. "The sun is clear above the horizon."

"No matter," I said, "it is a most magnificent spectacle, and we will see it do the rest of its rising, anyway."

In a moment we were deeply absorbed in the marvel before us, and dead to everything else. The great cloud-barred disk of the sun stood just above a limitless expanse of tossing white-caps—so to speak—a billowy chaos of massy mountain domes and peaks draped in imperishable snow, and flooded with an opaline glory of changing and dissolving splendors, while through rifts in a black cloud-bank above the sun, radiating lances of diamond dust shot to the zenith. The cloven valleys of the lower world swam in a tinted mist which veiled the ruggedness of their crags and ribs and ragged forests, and turned all the forbidding region into a soft and rich and sensuous paradise.

We could not speak. We could hardly breathe. We could only gaze in drunken ecstasy and drink it in. Presently Harris exclaimed:

"Why—nation, it's going *down!*"

Perfectly true. We had missed the *morning* horn-blow, and slept all day. This was stupefying.

Harris said:

"Look here, the sun isn't the spectacle—it's *us* —stacked up here on top of this gallows, in these idiotic blankets, and two hundred and fifty well-dressed men and women down here gawking up at us and not caring a straw whether the sun rises or sets, as long as they've got such a ridiculous spectacle as this to set down in their memorandum-books. They seem to be laughing their ribs loose, and there's one girl there that appears to be going all to pieces. I never saw such a man as you before. I think you are the very last possibility in the way of an ass."

"What have *I* done?" I answered, with heat.

"What have you done? You've got up at half past seven o'clock in the evening to see the sun rise, that's what you've done."

"And have you done any better, I'd like to know? I always used to get up with the lark, till I came under the petrifying influence of your turgid intellect."

"*You* used to get up with the lark—Oh, no doubt —you'll get up with the hangman one of these days. But you ought to be ashamed to be jawing here like this, in a red blanket, on a forty-foot scaffold on top of the Alps. And no end of people down here to boot; this isn't any place for an exhibition of temper."

And so the customary quarrel went on. When the sun was fairly down, we slipped back to the hotel in the charitable gloaming, and went to bed again. We had encountered the horn-blower on the way, and he had tried to collect compensation, not only for announcing the sunset, which we did see, but for the sunrise, which we had totally missed; but we said no, we only took our solar rations on the "European plan"—pay for what you get. He promised to make us hear his horn in the morning, if we were alive.

CHAPTER XXIX

HE kept his word. We heard his horn and instantly got up. It was dark and cold and wretched. As I fumbled around for the matches, knocking things down with my quaking hands, I wished the sun would rise in the middle of the day, when it was warm and bright and cheerful, and one wasn't sleepy. We proceeded to dress by the gloom of a couple of sickly candles, but we could hardly button anything, our hands shook so. I thought of how many happy people there were in Europe, Asia, and America, and everywhere, who were sleeping peacefully in their beds, and did not have to get up and see the Rigi sunrise—people who did not appreciate their advantage, as like as not, but would get up in the morning wanting more boons of Providence. While thinking these thoughts I yawned, in a rather ample way, and my upper teeth got hitched on a nail over the door, and while I was mounting a chair to free myself, Harris drew the window-curtain, and said:

"Oh, this is luck! We sha'n't have to go out at all—yonder are the mountains, in full view."

That was glad news, indeed. It made us cheerful right away. One could see the grand Alpine masses dimly outlined against the black firmament, and one or two faint stars blinking through rifts in the night. Fully clothed, and wrapped in blankets, we huddled ourselves up, by the window, with lighted pipes, and fell into chat, while we waited in exceeding comfort to see how an Alpine sunrise was going to look by candlelight. By and by a delicate, spiritual sort of effulgence spread itself by imperceptible degrees over the loftiest altitudes of the snowy wastes—but there the effort seemed to stop. I said, presently:

"There is a hitch about this sunrise somewhere. It doesn't seem to go. What do you reckon is the matter with it?"

"I don't know. It appears to hang fire somewhere. I never saw a sunrise act like that before. Can it be that the hotel is playing anything on us?"

"Of course not. The hotel merely has a property interest in the sun, it has nothing to do with the management of it. It is a precarious kind of property, too; a succession of total eclipses would probably ruin this tavern. Now what can be the matter with this sunrise?"

Harris jumped up and said:

"I've got it! I know what's the matter with it! We've been looking at the place where the sun *set* last night!"

"It is perfectly true! Why couldn't you have thought of that sooner? Now we've lost another one! And all through your blundering. It was exactly like you to light a pipe and sit down to wait for the sun to rise in the west."

"It was exactly like me to find out the mistake,

too. You never would have found it out. I find out all the mistakes."

"You make them all, too, else your most valuable faculty would be wasted on you. But don't stop to quarrel, now—maybe we are not too late yet."

But we were. The sun was well up when we got to the exhibition-ground.

On our way up we met the crowd returning—men and women dressed in all sorts of queer costumes, and exhibiting all degrees of cold and wretchedness in their gaits and countenances. A dozen still remained on the ground when we reached there, huddled together about the scaffold with their backs to the bitter wind. They had their red guide-books open at the diagram of the view, and were painfully picking out the several mountains and trying to impress their names and positions on their memories. It was one of the saddest sights I ever saw.

Two sides of this place were guarded by railings, to keep people from being blown over the precipices. The view, looking sheer down into the broad valley, eastward, from this great elevation—almost a perpendicular mile—was very quaint and curious. Counties, towns, hilly ribs and ridges, wide stretches of green meadow, great forest tracts, winding streams, a dozen blue lakes, a flock of busy steamboats—we saw all this little world in unique circumstantiality of detail—saw it just as the birds see it—and all reduced to the smallest of scales and as sharply worked out and finished as a steel engraving. The numerous toy villages, with tiny spires projecting out of them, were just as the children might have left them when done with play the day before; the forest tracts were diminished to cushions of moss; one or two big lakes were dwarfed to ponds, the smaller ones to puddles—though they did not look like puddles, but like blue eardrops which had fallen and lodged in slight depressions, conformable to their shapes, among the moss-beds and the smooth levels of dainty green farm-land; the microscopic steamboats glided along, as in a city reservoir, taking a mighty time to cover the distance between ports which seemed only a yard apart; and the isthmus which separated two lakes looked as if one might stretch out on it and lie with both elbows in the water, yet we knew invisible wagons were toiling across it and finding the distance a tedious one. This beautiful miniature world had exactly the appearance of those "relief maps" which reproduce nature precisely, with the heights and depressions and other details graduated to a reduced scale, and with the rocks, trees, lakes, etc., colored after nature.

I believed we could walk down to Wäggis or Vitznau in a day, but I knew we could go down by rail in about an hour, so I chose the latter method. I wanted to see what it was like, anyway. The train came along about the middle of the afternoon, and an odd thing it was. The locomotive-boiler stood on end, and it and the whole locomotive were tilted sharply backward. There were two passenger-cars, roofed, but wide open all around. These cars were not tilted back, but the seats were; this enables the passenger to sit level while going down a steep incline.

There are three railway-tracks; the central one is cogged; the "lantern wheel" of the engine grips its way along these cogs, and pulls the train up the hill or retards its motion on the down trip. About the same speed—three miles an hour—is maintained both ways. Whether going up or down, the locomotive is always at the lower end of the train. It pushes in the one case, braces back in the other. The passenger rides backward going up, and faces forward going down.

We got front seats, and while the train moved along about fifty yards on level ground, I was not the least frightened; but now it started abruptly down-stairs, and I caught my breath. And I, like my neighbors, unconsciously held back all I could, and threw my weight to the rear, but, of course, that did no particular good. I had slidden down the balusters when I was a boy, and thought nothing of it, but to slide down the balusters in a railway-train is a thing to make one's flesh creep. Sometimes we had as much as ten yards of almost level ground, and this gave us a few full breaths in comfort; but straightway we would turn a corner and see a long steep line of rails stretching down below us, and the comfort was at an end. One expected to see the locomotive pause, or slack up a little, and approach this plunge cautiously, but it did nothing of the kind; it went calmly on, and when it reached the jumping-off place it made a sudden bow, and went gliding smoothly down-stairs, untroubled by the circumstances.

It was wildly exhilarating to slide along the edge

of the precipices, after this grisly fashion, and look straight down upon that far-off valley which I was describing a while ago.

There was no level ground at the Kaltbad station; the railbed was as steep as a roof; I was curious to see how the stop was going to be managed. But it was very simple; the train came sliding down, and when it reached the right spot it just stopped—that was all there was "to it"—stopped on the steep incline, and when the exchange of passengers and baggage had been made, it moved off and went sliding down again. The train can be stopped anywhere, at a moment's notice.

There was one curious effect, which I need not take the trouble to describe—because I can scissor a description of it out of the railway company's advertising pamphlet, and save my ink:

"On the whole tour, particularly at the Descent, we undergo an optical illusion which often seems to be incredible. All the shrubs, fir trees, stables, houses, etc., seem to be bent in a slanting direction, as by an immense pressure of air. They are all standing awry, so much awry that the chalets and cottages of the peasants seem to be tumbling down. It is the consequence of the steep inclination of the line. Those who are seated in the carriage do not observe that they are going down a declivity of twenty to twenty-five degrees (their seats being adapted to this course of proceeding and being bent down at their backs). They mistake their carriage and its horizontal lines for a proper measure of the normal plain, and therefore all the objects outside which really are in a horizontal position must show a disproportion of twenty to twenty-five degrees declivity, in regard to the mountain."

By the time one reaches Kaltbad, he has acquired confidence in the railway, and he now ceases to try to ease the locomotive by holding back. Thenceforward he smokes his pipe in serenity, and gazes out upon the magnificent picture below and about him with unfettered enjoyment. There is nothing to interrupt the view or the breeze; it is like inspecting the world on the wing. However—to be exact—there is one place where the serenity lapses for a while; this is while one is crossing the Schnurrtobel Bridge, a frail structure which swings its gossamer frame down through the dizzy air, over a gorge, like a vagrant spider-strand.

One has no difficulty in remembering his sins while the train is creeping down this bridge; and he repents of them, too; though he sees, when he gets to Vitznau, that he need not have done it, the bridge was perfectly safe.

So ends the eventful trip which we made to the Rigi-Kulm to see an Alpine sunrise.